Praise for *Your American*

I could write volumes about Stan Miller and the tru...... ....
advisor he has become for me over the past twenty years. I won't do
that so you can jump right into reading his book. Stan has masterfully
crafted his forty years of serving affluent families into an elegant read and
detailed blueprint on how to positively impact your family and future
generations. This book does for the family what Stephen Covey's *Seven
Habits of Highly Effective People* does for the individual. You owe it to
yourself and your family to take these lessons on life and apply them.

Terry Dunken
Attorney at Law
Houston, Texas

In *Your American Legacy*, Stan Miller masterfully explains the most
powerful impact of wealth — the ability to create one's legacy — and shifts
the discussion away from the more mundane "task" of arranging for the
transfer of financial assets upon one's demise. Once understood, the focus
on legacy planning creates an opportunity for the lawyer to become the
"trusted advisor," and for the client to embrace planning as far more than
a "necessary evil" to transfer wealth, rather as an opportunity to make a
lasting impact on one's family and younger generations.

Howard S. Krooks, JD, CELA, CAP
Elder Law Associates PA
Boca Raton, Florida

With the lessons he has learned through his own life's invariable twists
and turns, together with those his clients and colleagues have entrusted
him enough to share, Stan Miller takes what blossoms in his heart as a
result and pours it into this treasure book for the rest of us, his readers,
to embrace and carry forward. After reading his words, you'll feel
moved to true passion for crafting a legacy of love, joy, honor, strength,
perseverance and hope, not only for yourself but for those whose lives
you are blessed to touch.

Helayne Levy Payne, J.D., LL.M.
Licensed in North Carolina and New York

Learn how to leave two Legacies: a financial legacy and a "Legacy of Virtue". Stan explains how in this ground breaking book by sharing powerful stories and experiences that Estate Planning is more than a will or trust. It is preserving your "Legacy of Virtue" your values, experiences and family history.

E. Lawrence Brock
St George Estate Planning
St George, Utah

Stan Miller totally GETS IT! He invites us to define who we are as a person, family member, patriot and inspires us to decide whether that definition equates to how others view us. His approach to self-awareness will help you create the foundation necessary to open the door to effective financial, legal and family planning and thereby capture and preserve what we hope our epitaph will say...OUR American Legacy.

Michael J. Amoruso, Esq.
President, National Academy of Elder Law Attorneys
Amoruso & Amoruso, LLP
Rye Brook, New York

If Stan Miller's book had been available to me, I likely would not have been estranged from my sisters for the last ten years. Most people, including me at one time, think that "estate" planning is for people with lots of money and property. That it's all about willing your "estates" after you die. That is an unfortunate myth that often results in hurtful arguments and estrangements in families; not to mention wasted dollars on litigation by one family member suing another. We've all seen it over and over again when a celebrity or famous wealthy person passes. What Stan painstakingly outlines and explains is that Legacy Planning is all about respect and love. Self-respect for your life's work, respect for those who may need to take care of your affairs in the event of disability and one of the most meaningful displays of love you can show to your family, friends, or any charity or institution you wish to honor. You won't find any legalese or complicated details in this book. You will find practical, step-by-step instructions on taking care of yourself and those you honor and love.

Roberta Trudeau-Epifanio
Principal, WealthCounsel, LLC
Reno, Nevada

King Solomon tells us that God has put eternity in the hearts of men (Ecclesiastes 3:11). We all have a desire to maintain a relationship with our Creator beyond this lifetime. Stan shows how we should develop this relationship now by reflecting lasting values through the estate planning process.

Stan draws on nearly 5,000 years of history when showing how fathers communicated timeless values to the next generation. Part 3 of the book connects the first two parts of the book with the conclusion by emphasizing ethical wills. Stan makes a strong case for why every family leader should supplement traditional legal documents with a statement of core values that can inspire commitment to transcendent ethical values across the generations.

Advisers need wisdom when encouraging heirs to respect lasting values. Stan has more than three decades of wisdom related to uncovering the deeper spiritual and relational issues undergirding strong estate plans. Our American legacy will be far stronger if our friends and family members, as well as their advisers, make earnest efforts to heed Stan's wise counsel. Then we can experience the clarity and joy that derives from using powerful strategies that instill lasting values for generations.

Tim Voorhees, JD, MBA, AEP®
Principal Partner, Family Office Law
Cost Mesa, CA

Stan Miller will make you rethink how one leaves assets on to their loved ones. A real eye-opener with real life practical examples of inspirational families who can ignite a new way of thinking about one's estate planning.

Vincent J. Russo, JD, LL.M, CELA★
Managing Partner, Russo Law Group
Long Island, New York

It was a pleasure to read *Your American Legacy.* I think it is what the world needs (not just America). Stan's common sense personal approach is meaningful to all ages and I wish that I would have had this guide earlier in life. This book should be read by young adults as well as those in the second half of life.

John Shickich
Partner, WealthMerge, LLC

This groundbreaking book, *Your American Legacy* blazes a trail to the next generation of estate planning, breaking through what many may view simply as a commoditized transaction into a unique and valuable process. Using illustrations and captivating historical stories, Stan describes three building blocks necessary to form a lasting legacy for you and your family. The lessons learned can be applied by estate planners and their clients alike, whether middle class or uber-wealthy. I strongly recommend this book, even if you've recently updated your documents.

Craig R. Hersch
Florida Board Certified Wills
Trusts & Estates Attorney, CPA and
Founder of The Freedom Practice™
Fort Meyers, Florida

I just finished reading with great enthusiasm "Your American Legacy". Hats off to the author on preparing such a wonderful explanation and overview of one's legacy whether wealthy or not. Just as he indicated in his book that in law school attorneys are taught by cases, so are Financial Advisors/ Planners in the various professional designation programs in our profession, i.e. The Certified Financial Planner®, the Chartered Life Underwriter®, etc. In most of the texts the cases we are given are higher net worth clients. This 4 part, 24 chapter book is a must read for all Certified Financial Planners® and Financial Advisors who assist their clients in the area of estate planning. This will add so much more to the practical side of their practices which is not obtained in the text books we use. The Parallel Inheritance Concept Stan Miller explains in this book is a phenomenal explanation on the why of legacy planning.

Dennis M. Axman, CLU, ChFC, AEP, CFP, RICP
Axman and Associates, LLC
Registered Representative/Financial Planner
Jacksonville, Florida

There are countless resources telling us how to plan for our finances and our estates. Mr. Miller gives us the spiritual and emotional motivation to systematically plan to be a better ancestor and citizen. I strongly encourage all who are looking to have intergenerational impact on the things that matter most to them to actively engage in reading this inspired book.

David K. Cahoone, Esq.
Senior Associate Director, Planned Giving Brown University
Westerly, Rhode Island

Generational planning and the transfer of our wealth are some of the toughest waters that we will navigate in our lifetime. All of the material things that we have earned, accumulated and worked hard for. How do we protect these things and then how to we insure that are wishes are fulfilled when we the time comes to ultimately give these things away? And then do our efforts help the ones we love, or undo them in ways we never could have imagined? It truly takes the help of someone like Mr. Miller, with his decades of Estate Planning experience, to guide us through these difficult questions. His book is often funny, sometimes alarming in the self-truths that are revealed, and always insightful into the deepest questions of planning for one's estate.

Jordan Theis
Trident Real Estate Investments, LLC
Orlando, Florida

A must read for any Financial Professional dealing with the subtle nuances of Estate and Legacy Planning and an excellent resource for anyone hoping to build a lasting Legacy that can inspire and inform future family members for generations to come.

Andrew Rodgers, CFP®, CHFC®
Mainspring Wealth Advisors, LLC
Bellevue, Washington

This book provides excellent guidance for those interested in legacy planning! Financial advisors should include these perspectives with all of their clients.

Brent Candebat, CHFC®, AAMS®
Pinnacle Insurance Consulting Group, Inc.
Edinburg, Indiana

As a financial literacy coach, I'm always looking for good resources to add to my toolbox. Having the discussion of not just building wealth but leaving a legacy of financial wealth and moral wealth is important. Stan Miller does a wonderful job with storytelling and sharing personal experiences to make this transition understandable for all groups. This is a must read if you're looking to build something that will outlive you. Thank you for sharing your wisdom Stan!!

Genein Letford
TEDx speaker & founder of Alumni360.Org
Los Angeles, CA

This wonderful book highlights the most important questions we can be asking in life and helps put first things first. For the millions of Americans who are looking to pass their stories and wealth down to future generations - what could be more important than family and family values? What could be more important than preserving those and being proud of your family heritage? The author captures these important elements and so much more. If you want to leave a legacy behind, read this book!

Kolton Thomas
Videographer
Little Rock, Arkansas

This book is useful for every adult or adult to be. It approaches the most avoided subject in life from the perspective of what we want most in life. Provides the perspective and tools needed to start and fulfill a lifelong journey of a family's meaning and legacy. Compelling stories make for swift reading. Our kids will read this before they get married.

Garth Hassel
East Idaho Insurance
Idaho Falls, ID

This book inspired me. Stan Miller has demystified the acts of planning one's estate, to giving of yourself freely and generously seeking nothing in return. It's encouraging to know we all have value to share and a legacy to leave.

John Franks
Real Estate Developer
Franklin, TN

I have always believed that legacy matters. This book helped me to outline my thoughts. Now I can put those thoughts into action. It is not all about making money. It is about passing values and traditions down to younger generations. That is cool stuff.

Christopher F. David
Entrepreneur
Arlington, VA

YOUR AMERICAN LEGACY

Powerful Strategies that Instill Lasting Values for Generations

PROVIDED BY
DENNIS B. SULLIVAN

Foreword
BY DENNIS B. SULLIVAN

Founder of the Estate & Asset Protection Law Center
of Dennis Sullivan & Associates

Your American Legacy represents the culmination of Stan Miller's work as an estate planning attorney for more than thirty years. In this book, Stan does not just highlight the singular importance of legacy planning as a means for attorneys and other professional advisors to connect with their clients. He takes it much further, by explaining in clear and concise terms the significance of engaging in a systematic process of how to plan for life and death, as well as for legacies, which may result in a life well lived now and for generations to follow.

Stan demonstrates that there are a series of building blocks to be followed when creating a plan that is driven by the focus of one's legacy. This represents a striking change from how legacy planning has typically been viewed in the past, which was to address legacy ideals *after* financial and legal issues have been dealt with by professional advisors or as a "feel good" exercise. In contrast, a more empowering approach for the planning process puts you and your legacy in the driver's seat, and it becomes the guiding principle for you and your family's financial, life, legacy and legal planning implementation and management decisions going forward.

This book is a result of Stan's significant personal and professional commitment to enhancing the process of estate, elder law, wealth strategies and asset protection planning. He encourages families, attorneys and advisors to create a more thoughtful and deliberate client-centered focus and forum. We have felt, for a very long time, that estate planning is a critically important process for advisors and the families we serve, and that it requires far more than a rudimentary understanding of legal principles.

Recently there has been tremendous growth of Wealth Counsel, our education and resource collaborative for estate and wealth strategies planning law firms. Our collaborative organization of estate planning and elder law attorneys is Elder Counsel. We are also members of the National Academy of Elder Law Attorneys. One of the reasons for this growth of our national organizations is they enable us to better serve as trusted family advisors to help people protect their home, spouse, family, legacy and life savings for generations.

The elevation of our role and responsibilities from draftsman to trusted advisor inevitably liberates both lawyer and client to think and talk about the truly important issues...including lifetime and legacy planning and protection. As Counselors at Law, CPA's, Estate, Elder Law and Wealth Strategies Planning Professionals, we have been blessed to have continuing opportunities to serve the planning, implementation and management needs of businesses, non-profits, institutions, individuals and Estates and Trusts as well as generations of family members since 1977.

In *The Millionaire Next Door*, author Thomas Stanley suggested that estate planning attorneys would have the most important role in our society in assisting in the transition of wealth among generations of family members. Stan Miller has committed himself not only to assisting in that transition, but also to thinking and talking about ideas such as the "Parallel Inheritance" concept which is the idea that given the choice, most would also like to leave a legacy of virtue rather than just a financial legacy.

This will inevitably lead to meaningful discussions between advisors and clients about legacy planning. Stan isn't the first person to explain the importance of one's legacy. Many have heard of and studied the significance of Maslow's hierarchy of needs as a way of explaining why we all yearn to think about the truly important matters and to reach a level of self-actualization.

The notion that there is something far more important to be imparted to family members than the mere transfer of assets is deeply embedded in the Judeo-Christian tradition. Ethical wills date back to the Old Testament and are intended to pass ethical values from one generation to the next. However, they are rarely used as a tool in modern American estate planning, which focuses on wealth rather than wisdom. If we want our heirs to be successful, we must find ways to impart wisdom, experience and values as well. We must transfer these intangible items such as initiative, responsibility and resilience, in addition to transferring assets through trusts and other legal devices. Part of legacy planning is helping families transmit those values in ways that will work. We have assembled a great collection of ideas and a path to implement those ideas for each and every one of our clients to make legacy planning the focal point of our estate plans.

A central finding of recent research into families is that parents should spend less time worrying about what they do wrong and more time focusing on what they do right. Planning your legacy and creating your family mission statement is a way to articulate what is important to you for your family.

Research has demonstrated the positive effects of family members working on their legacy and family mission statements for a few minutes daily or writing a description of their "best possible selves." The practice dramatically boosted their optimism, even more than expressing gratitude. Creating a family identity is the collective equivalent of imagining your best possible self. It forces you to conceive, construct, then place in a public place a written ideal of what you want your family to be.

This book empowers you and your family to take the necessary steps to build your own legacy plan! In so doing, you will achieve a sense of accomplishment, and your family will thank you for it for generations to come!

- Dennis B. Sullivan Esq, CPA, LLM, Ms Mgt
Wellesley, Massachusetts

Introduction

Your *American Legacy,* caught my attention immediately when I saw it at the National Symposium for Wealth Counsel, Estate & Wealth Strategy Planning Attorneys. We are making this book available immediately to all members of our Lifetime and Legacy Protection Program, as it speaks to a range of topics we find to be of utmost importance. Moreover, there has never been such an important time to do as much as you can to plan for health, disability, your life plan and legacy! We have been helping protect home, spouse, family, legacy and life savings for over 25 years. *Your American Legacy* introduces powerful concepts to help our clients protect those they love and all they have. You will discover a powerful process to enable you to protect your health, home, spouse, family, legacy, and life savings.

As part of our ongoing search for the latest and best ways to continue providing value to our clients now and in the years ahead, we are always educating and updating members of our Lifetime and Legacy

Protection Program. We accomplish this through a continuing commitment to education with seminars, newsletters, plan reviews and resources like this book! We believe it's vital for all people and families we serve to have the tools and education necessary so they can discover how to fix outdated plans or are motivated to create personalized plans that will work for their families now and in the years and generations to follow. This is so important because research shows 86% of trust and estate plans are outdated.

As you read through the 24 chapters, we hope you will discover significant insights for reviewing outdated plans as well as for creating new life, estate, elder law, or wealth strategy plans, based on you and/or your family's values, goals, aspiration and unique abilities and circumstances. Throughout *Your American Legacy*, you will discover powerful strategies that instill lasting values for generations to come. This valuable resource also provides concise explanations on a range of topics from estate plans to elder law and wealth strategies. Additionally, you will learn powerful concepts taken from Victor Frankl's *Man's Search for Meaning*, Abraham Maslow's *Hierarchy of Needs* and Dr. Thomas Stanley's book, *The Millionaire Next Door.*

Author, Stan Miller, has summarized so many of the important issues surrounding your legacy in this impactful book. As Victor Frankl explained, "you cannot control what happens to you in life, but you can always control what you will feel and do about what happens to you." Part of life and legacy planning is helping families address their values in ways that will work for them. How timely is the reminder of Victor Frankl's "wisdom for the ages!"

Several years ago, we watched Scott Fithian's Hollywood movie, *The Ultimate Gift*, based on the book of the same name by James Stovall. Soon thereafter, we discovered that Scott had passed away, much too soon, after a battle with cancer at the young age of only 45. More than 20 years ago he wrote a very enlightening book, *Values Based Planning*. He also created the Legacy Companies providing helpful client resources for professionals we work with, in our efforts to better serve the successful individuals and families we guide. Discovering Scott's premature passing inspired our team to discover even more about how we could better help the people and families we guide in even more meaningful ways. We wanted to support our clients to understand how important it is to be informed and how much they can do for themselves now and for generations to follow.

For more than 25 years, the Estate Planning & Asset Protection Law Center of Dennis Sullivan & Associates' mission was guiding families to discover where problems exist in their current plans as well as substantial opportunities for improvement. Our unique process enables families to discover, design, transform and manage their personal, family and business legacies for meaningful lives for themselves and generations to follow.

The purpose of Your American Legacy is to provide guidance, so you discover how to identify and pass on their values to your children, grandchildren, and others. For many these include crucial importance of education, being courteous, helping others, and giving back to their communities. These are the communities where they live, serve, recreate, prosper and share not just financial resources, but also talents and wisdom. Within each community there are causes and organizations that share our values and what we care about to pass on to our family and others in our community.

Organizations may include schools, neighborhoods, religious groups, inspiring individuals and non-profit organizations. *Your American Legacy* is a valuable collection of knowledge, insights and a path to implement these concepts to make legacy planning a reality for your own life, estate and legacy plans. We are pleased to provide you this exceptional resource. Please share *Your American Legacy* with your family, friends, and community, in the hope that you will be both inspired and empowered. We hope you will also be motivated to take the next steps to begin, review, create, protect and manage your own life and legacy plans now and in the years ahead. Count on our team's 25 plus years of experience with systems and resources like *Your American Legacy* to help you and your family discover how to find and create the right path for your family now and in the years ahead.

-*Dennis B. Sullivan Esq, CPA, LLM, Ms Mgt*
Legacy Advisor
Project Perseverance 501(C)(3)
Needham, MA
Founder of The Estate Planning & Asset Protection Law Center
of Dennis Sullivan & Associates

Table of Contents

PART III – THE THIRD BUILDING BLOCK: PROTECT THE THINGS THAT MATTER MOST

PART IV—FINIS: WHAT IS THE TRUE MEASURE OF SUCCESS?

Acknowledgements

I am tremendously grateful for the thousands of clients who have opened their hearts and their lives and allowed me to share in their hopes, fears, dreams, and aspirations. I am sure I have learned more from them than they have from me. I have received encouragement from my partners at WealthCounsel and ElderCounsel who reviewed early drafts of this book and offered constructive and encouraging comments.

I have also been encouraged by the attorney members and staff of WealthCounsel and ElderCounsel who generously shared stories from their professional practices and life experiences. We have an amazing network of professionals in this community. In this book, I frequently refer to strategies and practices I use with clients in my practice. Many of the solutions I provide my clients are strategies I learned from members of the WealthCounsel and ElderCounsel communities who deliver them as well as or better than I do. These are the people who continue to remind me that estate planning and elder law planning is far more than planning for the transition of material wealth. I am hopeful the ideas in this book will empower them to serve American families more effectively than they already do.

Finally, I must acknowledge my wife, Patrice Miller, and my niece, Sarah Fendley, who worked tirelessly to find resources and ideas that provide much of the substance of this book. This book would not exist but for their efforts.

Dedication

My wife Patrice Miller has been my partner in this project.
Without her patience, encouragement and assistance, this
book would never have been written. Together, we dedicate
this work to our sons, Matthew and Jonathan.
They are our legacy.

The Invitation

This book is my invitation to you to engage with me in thinking about your legacy. You have spent a lifetime working, saving, and learning. What you have and what you know, both good and bad, can inform and inspire others. By investing time and imagination, it becomes possible for you to take the sum of all your experience and the experiences of others that have been shared with you and create something that will endure far beyond your lifetime and empower the lives of people not yet born. I want you to see that this is possible; I also want you to see this as a joyful adventure.

In the first four chapters, I will provide you with a framework for how to think about your legacy in ways I hope are both understandable and practical.

"What you leave behind is not what is engraved in stone monuments, but what is woven into the lives of others."

—PERICLES, GENERAL OF ATHENS

Prologue

By Samuel T. Swansen Esq.

I first met Dennis Sullivan, along with Stan Miller and over 200 estate planning attorneys, when we were members of a national estate planning organization. We were introduced at the second, two-day session of our post-doctoral fellowship program. A number of us were collaborating to develop a unique process to help successful individuals and families uncover their core values, hopes and dreams. Together we designed a way to help people implement strategies to take control of their social capital to benefit the people and causes that are most important to them. Through these approaches and strategies, we have enabled numerous families across America to develop substantial legacies and meaning for their families, communities and causes that are important to them now and will continue to live on for generations to follow.

Soon after meeting Dennis, he introduced us to a Boston-based client who had a successful career in the financial service industry. This client had an elderly mother in the Philadelphia area where I live, and a family trust created in Pennsylvania in the 1960s with considerable funds in it. We have worked together for about twenty years to design and carry out an estate plan for this family. The trust document was old fashioned; in that the day, when the mother died, her estate would have picked up nearly $1M in taxable assets whether she withdrew them or not. We designed a charitable plan including a family foundation to create a charitable deduction that would offset the taxable assets and save the family some six figures in tax.

I bring this up because what I just described fits in perfectly with the title of this book *Your American Legacy* by Stan Miller. What Dennis and I accomplished together is at the very heart of what you are about to read in the coming pages. Namely why it is so important to put in place what is needed to leave your loved ones something of value.

Regarding the forementioned client story, a second problem was that the mother had received bad legal advice, which threatened to increase her death tax bill by a couple of million dollars. Dennis had the bold, even audacious, idea: *What if we undid the bad legal advice that the mother had received?* There was Pennsylvania law that permitted transactions to be unwound if based upon mistakes of fact or law, so we fixed the problem and time has proven that the solution worked! Meanwhile, it has taken 12 years after the mother died in 2008 for the full effect of the charitable deduction to play out.

This family reflects modern demographics in that the family size is shrinking: there are three children and only two grandchildren. This is where Stan Miller's book comes into the picture. Mr. Miller would advise us to note the family's desire to champion the work ethic of the grandchildren. He would say failing to do so, in favor of allowing them to realize all the money in this family picture, would stunt their character development.

The sole-acting trustee, under the charitable arrangement decided, to distribute the family foundation assets to a national financial services firm and create a Donor Advised Fund (DAF). This will reduce the paperwork in running a foundation and let charitable purposes go on. Someday their grandchildren will not have to write a personal check to charities, but rather can steer charitable gifts from the DAF to worthy causes in their communities. Nevertheless, they will not have funds that would permit them to stop developing their own careers and quit their "day jobs."

This particular client family's 20 year plus collaborative project with Dennis is winding down, but I leave with great admiration for his legal skills and creativity. Moreover, in a sense, it lives on because it is the continuing collaborative legacy of estate, elder law and wealth strategy planning professionals like Stan and Dennis and our colleagues from around the country who continue to devote their time and lives to the study, development and application of new and better ways to help the people, families and communities we serve. If you appreciate of the story presented above, you are about to discover some valuable insights and guidance in *Your American Legacy*! Take what I have shared with you here, together with Stan Miller's thoughtful approach to the subject, and start to build your own legacy for loved ones for generations!

- *Samuel T. Swansen, Esq.*
 Blue Bell, Pennsylvania

CHAPTER ONE

Your Legacy Matters

The Pilot's Story

He pushed the stick forward on his Grumman Wildcat forcing it into a nearly vertical dive heading straight into a formation of nine Japanese bombers that were barreling straight for the USS Lexington. It was a fluke that he had discovered the enemy planes. Someone had forgotten to top off his fuel tank, and he found the mistake just ten minutes into the flight. His flight leader insisted he leave the formation and return to the ship. It was on the route back to the Lexington that he saw the enemy planes below him.

The pilot didn't hesitate. Full throttle, he roared into the enemy formation. His wingman's machine gun jammed, so he was left with the only working gun. While tracers from the concentrated fire of the nine bombers streaked around him, he focused and took careful aim at the starboard engine of the last plane in the V formation and squeezed the trigger. Slugs from the Wildcat's six .50-caliber guns ripped into the Japanese bomber's wing, and the engine literally jumped out of its mountings. The bomber spun wildly into the South Pacific as the pilot moved to attack another enemy plane. He ran out of ammunition, but that didn't stop him—he quickly maneuvered to the other side of the formation and, using his plane as a weapon, smashed the port engine of another enemy plane.

1

The squadron commander learned what was happening and turned the squadron around to join the fight, witnessing three of the enemy bombers falling in flames at the same time. The pilot continued his diving passes as the enemy bombers flew into the defensive fire of the Lexington's anti-aircraft guns and released their bombs in a final attempt to destroy the carrier, which was maneuvering wildly to avoid the assault. They all missed.

In his solo assaults, the pilot destroyed five of the enemy planes and severely damaged a sixth. Miraculously, the pilot and his wingman both landed safely back on the ship. When film footage from his plane was developed, it became very clear what a truly heroic thing this pilot had done. With his gallant action—one of the most daring in the history of combat aviation—he saved the Lexington and the lives of the sailors aboard. He was awarded the first Medal of Honor given to a Navy fighter pilot in World War II.

The Lawyer's Story

Eddie was a Chicago lawyer. Everyone knew him as "Easy Eddie." He became famous, partly because he had cheated his client out of the patent rights to the mechanical rabbit used at greyhound race tracks. His corrupt reputation attracted him to the man who became his largest client—the famous gangster, Al Capone. Eddie became wealthy doing business with Capone.

In the process of becoming wealthy, Eddie also had a son. Those of us who have children know that they can impact us in ways that surprise and change us. In Eddie's case, he came to realize that his work with the Capone organization was not creating the kind of legacy—the reputational legacy—he wanted for his young son. Determined to do something about it, and knowing that the Capone organization would likely have him killed, Eddie became the key player in an IRS investigation that eventually resulted in Capone's imprisonment. In 1939, in a dark alley in Chicago, Eddie was gunned down. The crime has never been solved.

Eddie understood that his son was his legacy, and he did not want his son's reputation to be tainted by his own sleazy past. Eddie succeeded. His son was admitted to the U.S. Naval Academy, became a naval aviator and was deployed to the South Pacific in WWII. His son was Lt. Butch O'Hare, the pilot in the first story. O'Hare International Airport in Chicago is named in his honor.

Our Family is Our Legacy

Eddie's legacy saved the lives of thousands of sailors on board the Lexington and may well have altered the outcome of the war in the South Pacific. Eddie's legacy mattered then and it matters now. Your legacy matters too, and it can make an impact you cannot predict and may not even know about during your lifetime.

For most of us, our family is our legacy. We make our life count through our family. Family may be your children and grandchildren, but it could be other family members or people that are not biologically related to you but who matter to you just as much. You can define who your family is.

It is probably important to you that the people you call family grow to become productive citizens with a work ethic and a reputation for integrity. You want them to be financially secure. You want them to be good parents. You want them to be physically and emotionally healthy, have solid marriages, be free of drug or alcohol addictions and fully realize their unique potential. If you could find a way to do it, you'd like for your legacy to last, reverberate over time, and influence the lives of family members for generations.

If you want these things, you're in good company. Almost all of my clients tell me they want these things. If you're like the people I work with every day, you are looking for the wisdom and insight to accomplish these three objectives:

- You want practical strategies you can use to help you protect and instill lasting values in the people you love.

- You want to know you have done everything you can to be the best parent or grandparent you can be and to hopefully live long enough to see your success demonstrated in the lives of younger generation family members as they grow into adulthood.

- You want to know that by protecting, growing, and nurturing a strong family, you have helped make your community, the country, and the world a better place

If these outcomes are important to you, I believe you are in exactly the right place. I want to provide you with real strategies to make it easier to instill important, lasting values in younger family members. This book is not a theoretical treatise or an essay written only to create a feel-good moment. It is a roadmap filled with solid strategies you can start to implement right away.

This book was written especially for the parents, grandparents, aunts, uncles, godparents and mentors who take their role in the lives of the next generation seriously. You are my heroes.

★★★★★★★★★

Learn more about Lt. O'Hare in the resource links below. Lt. O'Hare was killed while on another combat mission shortly after the events I describe in this chapter. A permanent exhibit honoring his service is located in Terminal 2 at O'Hare International Airport in Chicago. The exhibit includes a restored Grumman F4F Wildcat like the one flown by Lt. O'Hare.

www.YourAmericanLegacy.com/resources

YOUR AMERICAN LEGACY

"Never doubt that a small group of thoughtful, committed citizens can change the world. Indeed, it is the only thing that ever has."

—Margaret Mead

CHAPTER TWO

The Time is Now to
Plan Your Legacy

Something Unique Has Happened in the Last Seventy-Five Years

This book was probably not needed seventy-five years ago. I believe it is needed now. There was a time before World War II, and for some time after the war was over, when grandparents and their grandchildren lived just down the street from each other. Sometimes they even lived in the same house. They had supper together several times every week. They worked the garden together. They celebrated birthdays and holidays together. They knew each other, and the family stories, history and legends—both good and not so good—got passed on informally and casually in the course of living.

Then things changed. World War II came along. When it was over, with the help of the GI Bill, Americans began attending college. The economy grew, and something that has never happened before began to happen in America—young people moved away from their family to take jobs in cities in other parts of the country. That trend accelerated into the new millennium, and now most grandchildren only see their grandparents a few times a year, if that often. Stories aren't shared. The relaxed closeness grandparents and grandchildren once experienced after school and during summer vacations has now become a brief couple of days between printing boarding passes and a rush to the airport in time to be back home and ready for work and school on Monday. This is how life is now. We know it well. What we don't realize is that—viewed in the arc of human history—this loss of generational connection is new. It has never happened before on any scale in the history of mankind. We haven't yet figured out the consequences of it, but there is no question there has been a loss of generational connection.

Moral Decline and the Loss of Generational Connection

In a May 2017 Gallup survey, eighty percent of a randomly sampled group of Americans surveyed concluded that America was experiencing moral decline.

It isn't news that Americans are politically polarized. Gallup wanted to know if political differences would impact the answers on this survey, so they asked respondents to self-identify as conservative, moderate, or liberal. It turns out that Americans from every point on the political spectrum generally agreed on the moral decline question.

My experience over the last thirty-five years of working with families has convinced me that there is a relationship between the loss of generational connection and moral decline. When we lose connection with who we are and where we came from, that space is filled with something else, and that something is often toxic. We see pointless, random violence in schools and in public venues such as in the 2017 mass shooting in Las Vegas, the deaths of seventeen students in Parkland, Florida in February 2018 and the death of eleven worshippers at a Pittsburgh synagogue in October of 2018. While the loss of generational connection is not unique to the United States, it is not happening in other countries to the same extent. In countries where generational connection is nurtured and valued, the consequences we see playing out in the United States are not happening.

I also believe there is a longing for generational *re*-connection. How else do we explain the success of *Ancestry.com* and *23andme.com*? Seventy-five years ago, we weren't that interested in reading stories about our ancestors. We lived down the street from them, we spent quality time with them, and on summer nights on the front porch after supper, we listened to their stories. That rarely happens now.

The Loss of Generational Connection has Consequences

This loss of generational connection comes with a price. When stories aren't shared, the values those stories communicate are also not shared. The rituals of holidays are also celebrated less often, and usually more casually. Technology has made communication easier, but I am doubtful that the things being communicated, at least inter-generationally, are the things that matter. It is a greater challenge today to grow children and grandchildren into civically responsible adults than at any other time in history.

I was on a flight recently with a businessman from Chicago. I discussed the increase in violence involving young people that is occurring almost daily in the inner city there. This man is active in the Chicago Jewish community. He celebrates Shabbat in his home with his teenage children every Friday evening. They attend the Synagogue on the Sabbath together as a family. I asked him how many of the young people he thought who were involved in violent crimes in Chicago were regularly participating in Shabbat on Friday evening with their parents. Not many, he speculated. Probably none.

Family Leadership is Where It Happens

It would be easy to say that the loss of generational connection and the problems it creates are bigger than any one of us or even government can solve. But I'm choosing to see it differently. I believe there is a solution and that we can all be a part of it. Families are the cultural unit where real change can happen. We may not have the clout to influence the outcome of legislation, but each of us does have the ability to bring proactive leadership to our families. That leadership can reconnect us to each other and to the traditions and time-tested values that make it possible for family members to live successful lives. We can also volunteer to mentor young people that don't have a family member to provide that proactive leadership. Instilling younger generations with the values we know are essential is how we grow our children into emotionally healthy adults. It is also the way we produce a real and positive change in our communities and in American culture.

You Don't Have to Be Wealthy

Most of the work that has been done in the legacy planning field has been focused on very high net worth families. I set out purposefully to make the solutions in this book accessible to everyone whether they are wealthy or just barely making ends meet. I want to democratize legacy planning. I am hopeful this book and the resources I have provided will motivate families at every place on the economic spectrum to take responsibility for defining and implementing their own legacy.

You Need a Framework and Strategies

You do need a framework for how to approach this important task, and you need to understand the strategies you can implement to make your legacy real and lasting. I think it's helpful if you know what others have done that has worked for them. It is much easier to start with a menu of possibilities and choose the strategies that are appropriate for your family. In this book, I offer you a full range of tools. There may be some that do not appeal to you, but you do not need to implement all of them. If you choose to only implement one of them and follow through seriously, that will be good enough.

I Want to Be Your Legacy Coach

As you explore the ideas you will discover in this book, I would like for you to think of me as your Legacy Coach. However, before you grant me that role in your life, you need to be sure I have the skills and insight that are authentically useful to you. I doubt you'd let a doctor perform surgery on you if you were not confident in his or her skills. For the same reason, you should know something about me before you take my advice seriously. So here goes: after growing up on a dairy farm in rural Arkansas, I graduated from Vanderbilt University Law School. I practiced law for ten years before deciding to focus my practice entirely on estate and business planning. That decision was life changing for me.

Based on my experience in law school, I thought the only thing estate planning attorneys did was spend their time fighting with greedy heirs. Every law school uses what is called the "case method" of teaching the law. In the class on Trusts and Estates, every case we studied involved a greedy, dysfunctional family. That's how the law school case method works. Law students study court cases. But to have a court case, there first had to have been a lawsuit or controversy that led to a court proceeding. We didn't study the estate plans of families that actually worked. We only studied the ones that did not work.

What I did not know until ten years after law school is that the greedy heirs' narrative reflects only a tiny fraction of the work estate planners do. Almost all my time is spent helping families protect the people they care deeply about—even those who have profoundly disappointed them—from risks that can be entirely avoided. I wish I had known that ten years sooner.

I made the decision to focus my practice to estate planning in 1986, just as the planning world began to recognize that the court supervised legal process known as probate could be avoided for almost everyone by using a revocable living trust rather than a will as the core of their estate plan. The idea of living trust-based planning was not popular at first. But it made so much sense to me that I continued to pursue it. After all, why should a family be forced to go through an expensive and time-consuming court process to transfer assets at death when that process could be accomplished much more quickly and with far less expense? I became a very public advocate of living trust planning and, for a time, I was on the receiving end of the enmity of older lawyers who saw me as threatening their livelihood from the lucrative probate work they anticipated doing when their clients passed away. Over time, things changed, and living trust planning became recognized by most estate planning professionals as the preferred estate planning solution. I'm proud to have been part of that revolution.

In 1997, a group of ten individuals, myself included, founded a company called WealthCounsel to provide education and technology support to estate planning attorneys in the United States. In 2008, WealthCounsel partnered with four of our colleagues who are nationally recognized elder law attorneys to create a new company called ElderCounsel, which provides similar education and technology solutions to the rapidly growing elder law attorney community. WealthCounsel and ElderCounsel are now the leading providers of education, technology and thought leadership for estate planning, elder law planning, and business planning professionals in the United States. These companies serve almost 8000 professional, committed attorneys throughout the country. These companies also provide a professional ecosystem that allows all of us to continuously share our best ideas and insights with each other. As a co-founder, director, and frequent speaker for these companies, I have ongoing interactions with an amazing network of members around the country, as well as financial advisors and other professionals who work in collaboration with our members. My work with these companies constantly infuses me with the best ideas in the planning universe, and many of those ideas are found in this book.

Because I also work with real clients in my private law practice every day, I am able to see first-hand how these ideas work in the lives of real people. I have represented several thousand individuals and families over the past thirty years, and I have been unfailingly supported in that work by my wife, Patrice. Patrice was pursuing her degree in Psychology and Special Education at Vanderbilt when we discovered each other at a campus cafeteria that featured cheap spaghetti on Thursday nights. She taught special education for eight years before becoming a full time mother, wife, and community leader. Patrice has been very engaged in developing and researching the ideas in this book. She is also the mother of my sons, one who left us in an automobile accident in 2004, and another who is creating his own legacy as an aviator in the United States Navy. Our experiences, both painful and positive, have provided us with a perspective that will allow us to be responsible mentors for you.

I have the very real expectation that the combined efforts of the several thousand professionals in the WealthCounsel and ElderCounsel attorney community, the professional financial advisory community, and the American families that choose to implement some of the strategies in this book will produce a positive change in the trajectory of American culture. Together, we have the power to be a catalyst that will produce a transformational shift leading to a return to civility and an increase in personal and community responsibility.

Common Ground

The people who read this book and connect with me through my website and on social media will be on all sides of the political spectrum. If they were all in the same room, they would find a great deal about which to disagree. Their interactions on political issues might be uncomfortable and even unfriendly. However, I also believe almost everyone reading this book can find common ground around the idea that when people are solidly grounded in their sense of self, and when individuals and families take responsibility for each other and their community, good things happen.

Actually, We Really Can Change the World

I don't think the possibility of positive cultural change is some delusional pipe-dream. In his book *The Tipping Point,* author Malcolm Gladwell taught us that a small number of the right people can move ideas from the confines of a small band of influencers to national, and even international, ubiquity. I choose to believe a few thousand of us—estate and elder law planning attorneys, financial advisors, parents and grandparents—can start to move the pendulum back to a more respectful, civil, and empowering common culture. Surely we can agree on that objective.

I know it can be done. I have seen transformational change occur as people band together to take responsibility for their future in my own hometown. I have seen it in families who decided things could be different and better. These things don't just happen, of course. They are the result of those who reimagine the future, and then—fueled by an empowering vision—take action to bring the transformation into reality. If enough of us take action to create positive change in our families and in our local communities, we won't have to worry about the future of our country.

None of what we want will actually happen until people take the first step to create positive change around them. My observation is that many people would like to create change in their families or their communities, but they never take the first step because they don't have a strategy or plan to follow. This book will hopefully reconnect you with your own motivation and then provide the practical resources you need to construct a legacy roadmap that is unique and empowering for every generation of your family. Prepare to be surprised when you discover how interested younger family members will be to engage in the legacy-building process with you.

I challenge you to join me and take the first step. Together, we can move mountains.

★★★★★★★★★★

Take a more in-depth look at the 2017 Gallup survey in the resource link below. You will also find the link to WealthCounsel.com and ElderCounsel.com where you can find a complete list of members organized by state, city and by zip code. We have also included links to other useful resources here.

www.YourAmericanLegacy.com/resources

YOUR AMERICAN LEGACY

"The greatest use of life is to spend it for something that will outlast it."

—William James

CHAPTER THREE

The Parallel Inheritance Concept

These Bold Italians Will Inspire You

The competition was fierce between the early Renaissance Italian city-states to build the world's most impressive cathedral. The beauty and grandeur of a city's cathedral defined its status in Medieval Europe, and also reflected its earthly competitive spirit. I share the story of this cathedral—the Duomo—built in the heart of Florence because I think it provides the perfect metaphor for us as we begin our legacy journey.

Rome had a head start with St. Peter's Basilica, but the Florentines imagined they could upstage Rome by building a cathedral with a dome that was much wider. However, the Florentines had a serious problem: the technology needed to construct a dome of the width and scale they wanted did not exist in 1296 when construction began. The Florentines did something that seems almost unthinkable today—they decided to begin construction of the lower portion of the cathedral and leave a giant hole in the ceiling, trusting that someone would eventually figure out how to build the dome. Eventually, someone did, and 140 years after the first brick was laid, the cathedral was completed. Even today, almost six hundred years later, the Duomo is still impressive and the dome is still the largest brick dome ever constructed.

The part of this story that inspires me is the willingness of community leaders to take the brave leap of faith to begin construction of a project they did not know how to finish and would never live to see completed. Our legacy is like that. We need to think big about it. We need to take the first steps to begin creating it even though we do not have all the answers available to us now.

Think of Your Legacy as a Construction Project

I have found it helpful to think about legacy planning as a kind of construction project. To build a structure that will last, someone first has to design it. When we have a plan, we can begin construction. But even after the construction starts, there are inevitable changes. Anyone who has built or remodeled their home knows that the house you build is never exactly like the one in the plans; even after construction is complete, there is maintenance. Responsible adults know that everything worth having requires maintenance. If we don't maintain things, they break down, become ugly and unusable. Building your legacy is like that too: you need to design, construct, and maintain. All three are required if we are serious about creating a legacy that will make a real difference in the lives of younger generations.

What is Your Legacy?

Not everyone will answer that question the same way. When most people are first asked, their answers usually focus on the money, property, farm or business they want to leave their family members when they die. That's reasonable. We spend most of our waking hours making a living and, hopefully, saving part of what we earn so that it will provide financial security for us when we need it and then pass what remains of it on to others after we're gone. The desire or impulse to leave a financial legacy is not only natural—it is desirable and honorable. We have an obligation to feed and clothe ourselves and to provide for our own housing and health care. If we have a spouse or children, most of us feel an obligation to provide for their support. It's a worthy objective to ensure that we and our family do not become a burden to taxpayers. So creating a financial legacy is something that is justifiably important. I offer some insights on the challenges to accomplishing that in Chapter Five.

When we think more deeply, we usually discover that we want our legacy to be more than the financial wealth we will leave behind when we die. We may want a part of our legacy to be expressed by the way we spend the rest of our lives here on earth, doing things that are satisfying and fulfilling, and doing them with the people and for causes that are important to us. The reality is that we have a very short time here, but with focus and thoughtful planning, we can do a lot in that very short time. What we do will not only have an impact now, it will impact how we will be remembered and how our lives will influence future generations. It will also impact the people we work with, the people we do business with, and the people we touch in our communities churches, synagogues, temples and mosques.

The Parallel Inheritance Concept

For many of us, our greatest opportunity to create something that transcends our financial legacy will be the impact we make on younger generations of family members. Most of my clients tell me their family is their most important legacy. That impulse is expressed in the desire to empower individual family members. It is also expressed in the desire to see the family unit remain solid and strong. These clients tell me they want their family to know its place in the community and to accept responsibility for making the community better. They also tell me how important it is for younger generation family members to have a connection to spiritual values. This may mean a connection to a particular faith tradition, but not always. Sometimes it is expressed as a desire that family members have a commitment to a set of values that include things like honesty, integrity, philanthropy and public service.

The measure of our success in creating that legacy is reflected in the qualities younger family members exhibit in their behavior. I have had many people tell me they want their children and grandchildren to have good "values." They see that as important because they realize values influence behavior. People tend to seek more of what they value. If our children value loyalty, honesty, and integrity, it is more likely they will act in a way that is consistent with those values.

There is a subtle distinction between the concept of "values" and the concept of "virtues." Virtues are behavioral habits—something that a person demonstrates fairly consistently. Virtues are what we do on a daily basis without thinking much about it. I believe I am a truthful person because I am honest in what I say and in the actions I take. Therefore, truthfulness is a "virtue" whereas honesty is a companion "value." The point I am making in drawing this distinction is that values point to virtues, and the thing we want our younger family members to possess are the specific values that drive virtuous character.

So, the second legacy that is important to consider is what I call a "Legacy of Virtue." With thoughtful planning, I believe it is possible to leave two legacies: a financial legacy and a Legacy of Virtue. With proper planning, it is possible to leave heirs both a financial inheritance and the values that empower them to use that financial inheritance wisely. Even if you have little or no financial inheritance to leave your heirs, it is still possible to leave a powerful and compelling Legacy of Virtue that can impact your family and community for generations after you're gone. Some of the greatest heroes in American history are individuals who possessed little financial wealth. The impact they made was entirely derived from the power of their demonstrated character. The idea that a financial legacy and a Legacy of Virtue are accessible for individuals and families is what I call the concept of "Parallel Inheritance," and most of the people I work with tell me they would like to have both.

I believe you can have—and pass on—a financial legacy and a Legacy of Virtue. The time to start building both of those legacies is now. Trust your instincts and take bold action. As you move forward, the people and the resources to help you build your legacy will begin to appear in your life. The leaders of Florence were right—think big and begin even when you don't have it entirely figured out and even though you know you will not live to see it finished.

★★★★★★★★★★

Learn more about the remarkable Duomo that today remains the central architectural feature of Florence. You can also meet Filippo Brunelleschi, the architect that successfully developed the design for the dome.

www.YourAmericanLegacy.com/resources

YOUR AMERICAN LEGACY

"Are we being good ancestors?"

— JONAS SALK

CHAPTER FOUR

A Planning Model for the Twenty First Century

From Mexico to Maslow

Because I have asked you to think of building your legacy as a construction project, I wanted the conceptual model we use for that project to be the most stable structure in the world. The structure that best captures the ideas in this chapter and in the remaining chapters of this book is the pyramid. The stability and durability of the pyramid has been proven over time by the Egyptians, the Mayans, and the Aztecs, all of whom built pyramids that have survived for thousands of years. We also know that pyramids are not a single, solid block. We have all seen pictures that show how they were constructed from carefully hewn blocks of rock, stacked one on top of the other over time with considerable effort. The image of the pyramids and the insight of what we know about how they were constructed provide us with a useful way to think about how we construct our own legacy.

The pyramid that provides us with the most useful framework to think about our legacy is not found in Egypt or Mexico. It is the pyramid inspired by psychological theorist Abraham Maslow:

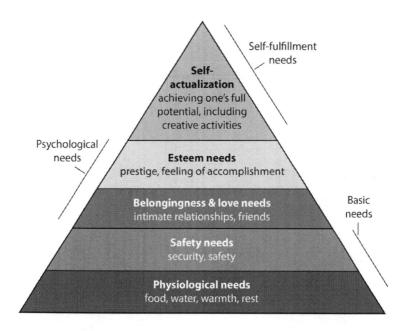

Professor Maslow gives us a way of looking at human needs in the order in which they must be met. His model recognized how difficult it is for humans to think about self-esteem and self-actualization until they have food, clothing, and a place to sleep. He calls this the "hierarchy of needs," and I have found this hierarchy of needs to be relevant in understanding a person's readiness to participate in legacy planning. In my experience, before someone is open to thinking about their lifetime legacy or the legacy they want to leave behind when they die, they first want to know they have made provision for their most fundamental needs. They want to know they can put food on the table, make the house payments, afford a doctor, and retire with dignity. As they age, they also want to know they can pay for the cost of long term care.

When I sit down with clients who work in high-risk professions, the first topic they want to discuss is how to avoid losing what they have if someone files a lawsuit against them. Nothing else matters until they know I can protect them from the risk of losing their life savings. Almost all my clients want to provide an estate planning structure to protect their young children, and it's not uncommon for us to have emotional conversations with our clients about how to design a structure to protect adult children that do not handle money well or who have drug or alcohol addictions. Sometimes, it is important to ensure their child with special needs will qualify for government-funded benefits, including health care programs, and still have resources available to enjoy a basic quality of life.

The Legacy Planning Pyramid™

Financial planning and estate planning are usually viewed as separate, stand-alone activities. I want to change that mindset. I want all of us to begin to understand that the most powerful outcomes, the outcomes that satisfy our clients deepest needs, are interconnected. I developed the Legacy Planning Pyramid ™ as a tool to help us reimagine how we think about the planning process. This is the model I use now with all of my clients to help them understand the sequence of action steps they must take to secure their financial future, protect the assets they have earned and saved and to protect the non-financial wealth—the legacy—they want to pass on to younger generations. It looks like this:

THE LEGACY PLANNING PYRAMID™

LEGACY

FINANCIAL

LEGAL & TAX

The Legacy Pyramid ™ provides us with an expanded framework for understanding how we plan, and it drives a process that allows us to actually implement solutions that produce the best results over time. The Legacy Pyramid ™ expresses the concept that proper planning is not a financial plan, an insurance product or a set of legal documents. Legacy planning encompasses all of those things. However, it cannot be pulled apart from financial planning, and it cannot be severed from the foundational legal solutions that provide basic protections every family must have. Legacy planning is all of those things fused into a thoughtful, unified whole and delivered by professionals who understand their own limitations and who know they must bring other professionals into a coordinated process if the results are going to be real and lasting.

The Order-Taker Mentality and Why It Rarely Works

There is a tendency among professionals to reflexively deploy the tools, skills or products they know best. You may have heard the old expression: "If the only tool you have is a hammer, the whole world becomes a nail." A surgeon friend of mine shared a common aphorism used among surgeons: "To cut is to cure." Estate planning professionals frequently fall into the same trap, and it rarely produces solutions that meet our clients' deepest needs.

Too frequently, the estate planning attorney functions as an order-taker to clients who make specific requests for solutions they may have heard or read about. It is very common, for example, for clients to make an appointment with an attorney to have their will made. Quite often, that attorney will comply with the client's request and make them a will. That seems reasonable, right? But if you look closer, you discover that a common reason clients want to have their will made is to avoid a court supervised probate process and simplify the settlement of their estate. Wills clearly don't accomplish that outcome: they actually guarantee that the estate will require a time consuming and expensive probate proceeding.

I now see this same order-taker mentality happening with clients who come in requesting living trusts. Perhaps they saw an advertisement for living trusts on television or went to a seminar where living trusts were promoted. Living trusts are great planning tools, but they don't accomplish every planning objective, and quite often, they don't accomplish the very objective that brought the client to the lawyer. This happens even more frequently when an online legal document generating company provides the solution. If you go to Legal Zoom or Rocket Lawyer and purchase a will, you will get a will, whether or not a will accomplishes the outcome you wanted. Quite often, it doesn't.

Financial advisors quite properly understand that clients want their money securely managed or need insurance to protect against a risk. Even now, it is only the most enlightened financial professionals who look beyond the specific insurance or investment solution they just sold the client to consider whether or not that solution is properly integrated into the client's estate planning structure.

Planning should be driven by the objectives our clients want to accomplish—not the tools we can efficiently produce. Accomplishing those objectives almost always requires collaboration with other professionals.

Do the First Things First

In the same way that Maslow recognized that survival and safety needs must be addressed first, I understand that a financial and legal plan must also be implemented first. Only then can we move up the hierarchy of needs to reflect on the meaning of our lives and consider the myriad of ways we will choose to communicate that meaning to younger generation family members. Our personal legacy plan must be constructed block by block by doing the first things first and following through. Planning professionals cannot focus on the one thing they know how to do and only implement that component—they must see their clients as whole persons who need an integrated set of solutions. They must work collaboratively with other professionals who know how to do the other things.

The Legacy Pyramid ™ forces us to expand our skill set and our network of relationships, and our clients are better off for it. Professional satisfaction comes when we can clearly see we are solving the problem and not merely a piece of it—that we are not providing a solution for a moment in time, but for all time.

Allow yourself to be inspired by the enlightened lesson of the Florentines 600 years ago and choose to begin your own legacy journey by taking the steps to lay the foundational building blocks of your legacy plan. Trust that you can do magnificent things even if you don't fully know how you will do them. Proceed with the certain knowledge that the best expression of your effort may only be fully realized in the years after you are gone.

In the remaining chapters, I take each of the three elements of the Legacy Pyramid™ and explore them in detail.

★★★★★★★★

Learn more about the pyramids constructed by the Egyptians, the Mayans and the Aztecs. The stability and durability of these ancient structures inspired me to use the pyramid as the conceptual model of the structure I use to help my clients preserve and protect both their financial and non-financial wealth. I have also provided a link to an explanation of Maslow's Pyramid: this widely recognized model of human needs provides the inspiration for the Legacy Planning Pyramid™. I have also included a reference to **Entrusted: Building a Legacy that Lasts** *by David R. York and Andrew L. Howell, an excellent recent book that takes a slightly different point of view on to how to approach building your legacy.*

www.YourAmericanLegacy.com/resources

PART 1

The First Building Block:
Create Your Financial Legacy

U nless you are a monk who has taken a vow of poverty and are willing to rely entirely on the generosity of others, financial resources are essential to your survival. But I'm guessing you do not want to merely survive. You want to thrive. When you are financially secure, you can take care of your own needs and enjoy an abundance you can share with others. Learning how to create that abundance by building your own financial security is the first building block of your legacy. In the next three chapters, I share insights on how you can build that financial legacy.

"You must gain control over your money, or the lack of it will control you."

—Dave Ramsey

Y O U R   A M E R I C A N   L E G A C Y

*"He who wishes to be rich in a day
will be hanged in a year."*

– LEONARDO DA VINCI

CHAPTER FIVE

Create a Solid Financial Plan

The Mystery of the Golden Ball

I was awestruck as I stood on the eighty-fifth floor of Taipei 101 in the heart of Taiwan's capital city. I was not looking at a view of the city, but through an interior glass window at a gold metal ball that weighed 730 tons. It resembled a giant golden egg. This metal ball was resting in a supporting sling device made of metal cable material. Taipei is very earthquake prone, and this building, which was for a brief period in the early 2000's the tallest building in the world, would swing uncomfortably when an earthquake struck if it were not for this golden ball. The ball was designed to swing in the opposite direction of the natural sway of the building and serve as a counterweight that would retard the building's movement.

The question on my mind was this: How did they get a 730-ton ball hoisted to the 92nd floor? That seemed like an impossible task. I was sure there was no crane in Taiwan or anywhere in the world that could hoist a ball that heavy. I explored further and learned some things about the engineering of this amazing building that can also help us learn a thing or two about building our financial legacy. What I learned was that the ball was not hoisted to the top of this structure. Actually, forty-one separate sheets of metal were hauled one by one to the top of the building and then welded together to create what we now see as one golden, egg-shaped ball.

It was created carefully, patiently, piece by piece over time. This seems like a good metaphor to inform our thinking about how to create our own golden egg of financial security.

A Lottery Ticket is Not a Financial Plan

Financial planning is not buying lottery tickets every week. It is not some secret strategy known only to a fortunate few that will create financial security instantly or overnight. I know people who are still counting on luck to rescue them from their own failure to plan. Unfortunately, the media makes it a lead story when someone wins a Powerball drawing, thus enabling the fantasy that we can be rescued from our own financial immaturity in one glorious moment. Financial planning is a thoughtful activity that includes saving, investing, and not losing our money. It is not created by luck or magic. Most of us do not have the knowledge and skills to do it well, but with some professional help and the application of basic discipline pursued over time, we can all build a real measure of financial security that will allow us to live through retirement in dignity, be able to educate our families and fund our own health care costs.

Financial Security is, on Balance, a Good Thing

Thoughtful and responsible financial stewardship is the key to a quality of personal freedom that is only available to people who want to live their lives the way they choose, without being limited by the boundaries imposed by scarcity or the bureaucratic limits of government programs.

Individuals who live their life practicing the habits and discipline of positive stewardship find they have the freedom to move about the world as they choose while also practicing generosity with family members that are less fortunate. And they can support causes that matter to them.

The capacity to live an abundant life does not require financial wealth. I know monks who have taken vows of poverty and live very fulfilled lives. We all know people who are poor who inspire us with their joyful presence. Rosa Parks and Mother Teresa are just two examples. But for most of us, engaging with the world in the way we would like requires financial resources. Educating our children and grandchildren the way we would like requires financial resources. Travel can expand our children's world view and allow them to understand and appreciate people who are very different. But travel, even with just a backpack and a rail pass requires financial resources. Providing the maximum range of choices for our own health care requires financial resources. I think Maslow got it right when he recognized that—for most of us—the capacity to satisfy basic personal needs is a precondition to satisfying our loftier needs and desires.

I believe the world would be a better place if more individuals and families were financially secure and independent. Marriages are more stable and happier when the couple does not have the pressure of financial stress. Children are healthier and more emotionally well-adjusted if they are raised by parents who are not in a constant state of financial difficulty. People tend to be healthier and live longer if they are financially independent. Charities of all kinds exist because people with resources are willing to share their abundance. Yes, financial security can be a good thing.

Are You Wealthy?

This chapter is for two distinct groups of people—those who are wealthy and those who are not. For those who are not, there is clearly a greater focus on growing assets and income. But the financial issues for both are surprisingly similar. I have explored the issue of wealth with almost every client I have served over the last 30 years—that's thousands of clients—and very few of them have described themselves as wealthy. Almost every client I have served has what I call "first generation wealth." That is, they started with nothing and built what they have over time. Measured by the standard of most middle class people, it may be quite a lot. But to those clients, wealth did not arrive suddenly and without struggle. Even the adult children of first generation wealthy parents are old enough to recall the struggles their parents had in the earlier, less prosperous times. For these clients, their wealth has accreted over time and does not seem like that much. When I add up the value of what they have, it's very common for them to challenge me, claiming that I have overstated the numbers. They almost always live a lifestyle that is far below what their current income would allow.

The Millionaire Next Door Got It Right

My insights on this topic are quite similar to the more methodical and scientific findings of Thomas J. Stanley in his best-selling book, *The Millionaire Next Door*. In this book, Stanley tells the story of an occasion in which he invited a group of wealthy people to an event he sponsored which was connected to his research on the lifestyles of the wealthy. He provided caviar, expensive wine, and elegant hors d'oeuvres. He noticed that almost without exception, the people he invited seemed uncomfortable and out of place. He discovered that most of them were embarrassed to admit they didn't know what to do with these unfamiliar foods. Most of them lived in the same middle class neighborhood where they had lived for decades and drove cars like the ones they drove in their younger, more cash-challenged days. The opulence Stanley thought he'd find was not at all familiar to these people, even though at that point in their lives, they could well afford it.

My own experience with my clients completely validates the findings of Stanley's research. It is very common to have clients tell me in their initial meeting that they don't really have that much. They tell me they assume I usually work with people that are much wealthier than they are. When I've asked them to define what it means to be wealthy, I have received uncannily similar answers—it is about three times what that client has in net worth. I was supervising the signing of a set of complex estate planning documents several years ago for a couple that had $25M in net worth. As we were wrapping up the signing, the husband asked me this:

"Stan, what do you do for clients that are wealthy?"

"What do you mean?" I asked.

"Well—you know—what do you do for those people with $75M or $80M dollars?

There it was, three times what they had. I get almost the same answer from clients that have a net worth of $500,000—wealthy, to them, is a person with $1.5M or $2M in net worth.

When I think of what it means to be "wealthy," I think of it this way— do I have enough income from secure sources without working (because I may have a health issue that prevents me from working), to allow me to provide for myself and the people who rely on me so that all those basic needs can be met, and have funds left over to provide for the things I want to do during my life without being concerned about running out of money? That income may come from retirement pensions or Social Security; it may come from real estate rental income, from a business, or dividends from a securities portfolio. I have clients with $500,000 in net worth who are wealthy by that definition. I have clients with a $20M net worth who are not wealthy by that definition. If your needs include vacation homes in warm climates or private jets, the net worth you need to be *wealthy* is going to be higher.

What is Your Number?

Regardless of how old you are or where you are on your journey to financial independence, you have two numbers—an income number and an asset number. Your income number is the amount of recurring income you need to pay your monthly bills, pay for vacations and dinner out, and making the charitable contributions you want to make while you are living. Your income number will take into account income that is generated from sources unrelated to your assets—such as retirement pensions and Social Security.

Your asset number is the value of the invested assets you have that produce recurring income—things like dividends, interest or rental property. These are the assets that generate the cash you need to provide your income number without spending the asset itself.

For all individuals and families, your number should consider these four distinct needs for resources:

Your Basic Lifestyle Needs. The income you need to maintain the quality of life you want for yourself and for your family both now and when you are older, when long term care costs become an issue.

Personal Enjoyment. The income you need to pay for travel and fine dining. You may want to purchase assets for your personal enjoyment such as boats, vacation homes, or airplanes. These assets are not income generating assets: usually they have to be insured and maintained, so they consume income.

Entrepreneurial & Charitable Opportunities. You may want to have resources to fund entrepreneurial opportunities for yourself or family members and to make charitable contributions.

Emergency Funds. Most of us want to have ready cash we can access quickly if an emergency arises. I have found that it is very common for clients to have an outsized need for emergency funds. I frequently see clients of modest means keeping $200,000 or more in cash accounts or certificates of deposit earning almost no interest simply because it makes them feel better to have those funds within reach on short notice.

It's important to know your number. Without it, you are shooting in the dark. We have served clients who actually saved enough to hit their number and didn't know it. Imagine their surprise when they discovered they could retire right then and spend the rest of their lives doing what they wanted with the people they cared about the most. Most financial advisors I know believe assets can be safely invested in a diversified portfolio of marketable securities that will allow 4% or 5% of the value of the account to be consumed each year for an indefinite period into the future. That concept assumes the account actually generates a net return of 6% to 8% each year, and the excess growth is reinvested so that, over time, it provides a hedge against inflation that preserves the buying power of the 4% or 5% you actually take out each year.

How to determine your asset number:

- Calculate the total annual income you will need in current dollars.
- Calculate the annual income you have (or expect to have) from retirement pensions, Social Security, and other non-asset based or work related income sources.
- Subtract the non-asset based income from the income you determined you need. If your non-asset based streams of income are not enough to provide you with the total income you need, then divide the total annual amount of the shortfall by 4% or 5%. The resulting number is your second number—that is, the dollar value of investible assets you will need to maintain your lifestyle as you have defined it.

When you are calculating your asset number, be sure you consider the cost of long term care you may require in the future. This may increase the value of the assets you will need to maintain your lifestyle without depleting them.

Your numbers—both your income number and your asset number—are your destination. If you don't know your numbers, you will not know how you are progressing or know when you arrive. Over the next two chapters, we will look at some strategies that will empower you to reach your number.

★★★★★★★★★★

Learn more about the innovative golden ball located at the top of Taipei 101. Just as our financial reserves provide financial security for us, this golden counter-weight has proven to be an effective device to reduce the effect of the frequent earthquakes that impact the island of Taiwan. I have also included the reference to several very useful book and other resources on the subject of wealth-building.

www.YourAmericanLegacy.com/resources

YOUR AMERICAN LEGACY

"Rich people believe 'I create my life.' Poor people believe 'Life happens to me.'"

— T. HARV EKER, AUTHOR OF
SECRETS OF THE MILLIONAIRE MIND

CHAPTER SIX

The Three Core Principles of Wealth Building

A Life Lesson from a Multi-Billionaire

Dan Duncan was born into a poor family in East Texas. His childhood was marked by tragedy—his mother and his brother died when he was seven. He was raised by his grandmother. In 1968, Mr. Duncan started his business with $10,000 and a truck. By 1973, his company was worth $3 million and by the late 1970s, his company had become successful enough to obtain a $300 million line of credit from a bank. Mr. Duncan built several pipeline companies that moved oil and gas around the country. When he died in 2010, he had a net worth the Wall Street Journal estimated at more than Twelve Billion Dollars. Not bad for an accountant from East Texas. I share Dan Duncan's story here not because he was rich, but because of the way he became rich. I often hear people tell me that to become wealthy, you have to cut the sharpest deals, be the toughest negotiator, squeeze every penny out of every deal and take unscrupulous advantage when you have the opportunity. This is a common myth that is widely-accepted by people who are not wealthy and believe they never will be wealthy because they would not want to become that kind of person.

Dan Duncan didn't buy into that myth. As the Wall Street Journal put it, Mr. Duncan "cultivated a reputation for square deals." In an interview with the Houston Chronicle, he summed up his approach to business: "In this business, everyone has the same product. What's unique, besides your assets and staff, is your relationships. If you earn people's trust, you'll receive the first call when they want to make a deal." A close friend of Mr. Duncan's described him as a guy who "......believed the key to success in a transaction was making everyone a winner." Dan Duncan is a hero of mine precisely because he proved that good guys can finish first.

I have worked with many successful business owners in my career. I can count on one hand the number that approached their business as the tough, hard, scorched-earth negotiator. For some of those who did, success was usually a short term experience followed by bankruptcy. Almost all of my business-owner clients have been unfailingly honest in their dealings and fair to their employees, their customers and business partners. Of course they pay attention to business and are careful to spend resources wisely. But they also contribute time and money to their community and to charity.

If you have not yet achieved financial security for yourself, I want to be clear that you can do it without compromising your personal integrity or transforming yourself into some kind of unsavory dealmaker. In this chapter, we look at how you can achieve financial security for yourself and your family.

Financial Independence is Possible

You can become financially independent if you make the decision to practice certain basic principles. These principles can be learned and implemented by anyone. One of the secret benefits to being an estate planner is that we get the real, inside information on our clients. We have the unique opportunity to see what works and what doesn't. I've come to regard this as an incredible benefit to my line of work, and one that I never anticipated. While working with clients who have enjoyed financial success,

I have seen specific patterns that can be reduced to a set of three core principles that can be learned and replicated by anyone. Here they are:

1. Don't Lose What You Have
2. Don't Spend All You Earn; Invest the Excess Thoughtfully and Systematically Based on a Plan
3. Be Wary of Debt, and Avoid Consumer Debt Entirely

The journey to financial independence begins where you are now, but with a roadmap that has successfully guided others to the destination of financial security. If you have not arrived at that destination, it's not too late. In this chapter, I will provide you with some guidance and insight that has been proven over time to work effectively. I have also provided a useful collection of resources you can refer to when you are ready to seriously focus on creating your own financial plan.

Core Principle Number One: Don't Lose What You Have

The first rule of financial success is to make certain you are not at risk of losing what you have. Many years ago, a wise and very wealthy client decided to share with me his secret to financial success. I also learned that he went through a business and personal bankruptcy several years earlier because he had violated the rules he was about to share with me—the advice he was volunteering had been learned the hard way. Here is what he told me: "Stan," he said, "you can risk your time. You can risk your interest. Never, under any circumstances, risk your principal. It's that simple. If you have your principal, you can recover. If you don't, you have to start over from scratch. That's difficult and takes a very long time." Thinking back, I'm still flattered that he was thoughtful enough to volunteer advice this valuable. I also think about how much better off financially my wife and I would be if I had consistently followed his advice.

For most of my clients, it has taken a long time and hard work to get where they are, and they would like to go to bed at night without the fear of waking up tomorrow and being forced to start over.

This is not an irrational fear. I had a client a few years ago who was living a financially secure and comfortable retirement, golfing several times every week, and traveling to see his grandchildren several times a year. He learned of a new bank that was offering significantly higher returns on certificates of deposit—the returns were not only higher; they were substantially higher. It turned out that the bank that issued these financial instruments was running a Ponzi scheme. The owner of the bank is now serving a very long federal prison term. Our client was very fortunate that the church he attended agreed to hire him as the janitor. While this was not the job he imagined he'd have at age eighty, it did pay him enough to allow him and his wife to stay in their home.

This risk of losing what you have is also present when too great a percentage of your assets are in one or a small number of securities. I remember the sudden implosion of WorldCom and Enron; both of these companies appeared to be thriving and successful—until they weren't. Almost no one on Wall Street saw their downfall coming. Every adult American with an investment account painfully recalls the gnawing, frightening feeling of watching the stock market implode in 2008 and 2009. In that collapse, the S&P 500 declined by 35%. In the recovery that followed, we learned that it takes more than a 35% rebound in the market to offset a 35% decline.

Many of my clients are doctors. My first conversation with a doctor will always be about how to protect the assets that he or she has accumulated if they are sued for malpractice. The number of malpractice cases filed against doctors in my part of the country is not that great— the prevalence of litigation against doctors on the East and West coast is actually much greater. But that doesn't matter. When it happens to you, the statistics aren't relevant. These clients have a visceral fear that everything they have worked for will be taken away by a jury who couldn't possibly understand the complexities of the decision-making process that went into the diagnosis and treatment of a patient.

44

I also hear business owners express their fear of losing everything they have worked for to a runaway jury composed of individuals who have never had to make a payroll. They understand that even if they ultimately win the lawsuit, the loss of their business reputation, the time required to defend a lawsuit and the money required to pay the lawyers to represent them will be a massive drain on their personal wealth. The good news is that it is possible to effectively prevent a catastrophic loss from litigation through a combination of insurance coverage and the thoughtful structuring of asset ownership in limited liability companies and special kinds of trusts. While it is true that the risk of being sued is increasing, it is equally true that the tools available to protect assets from the risk of loss from litigation are more powerful and more available than they have ever been.

Younger Families Have Unique Risks

In younger families, one or both spouses probably work. Hopefully their income is adequate to fund all their lifestyle costs, provide for their children's education, and leave a cushion for saving, investment and trips to Disney World. If one of them dies, the calculation becomes much more complicated as the survivor still has to figure out how to take care of the children while he or she continues to work. Unlike a few decades ago, today's grandparents are usually not close enough to be truly helpful. So, when I look at the asset number for a young family, there is almost always a shortfall. Unless there are wealthy parents ready to step in, that shortfall can only be filled with life insurance.

For adults in their 30's and 40's, term insurance is very inexpensive on a cost per $1000 of death benefit basis, so I am proactive in encouraging these clients to get an inexpensive life insurance program in place. My advice for every young household is to calculate how much income would be needed to support the household if one spouse died. Then, I calculate how much we would need to increase the asset base to produce this amount of income indefinitely, assuming the asset base could consistently deliver a 4% or 5% cash distribution to the household every year. We also assume the asset base will grow over time, so the family has protection from inflation. For example, if the shortfall is $60,000, I recommend that a couple purchase $1,500,000 of term life insurance on the breadwinner spouse. If both spouses are employed, this calculation needs to be done for each spouse and insurance purchased for each of them in an amount sufficient for the income earned from the invested life insurance death benefit to replicate the earnings of that spouse.

The Single Greatest Threat to Middle Class Families

As couples get older, they have to consider the risk that one or both of them will need home health care or spend time in a nursing home. This fear comes up in almost every client meeting I have with middle class clients. They don't want to run out of money before they run out of life. Being broke and dependent entirely on the generosity of others or your state's Medicaid or MediCal program is a legitimate fear, and one that should motivate you to plan now to eliminate this risk. There are great solutions, but they work better and cost less the sooner you take action.

I believe this is the greatest risk that looms over middle class American families. Data now suggests that there is a 70% likelihood we will spend some time in a nursing home before we die. The cost of long term care varies from state to state. In the south, the cost in 2018 ranged from $5,000 to $6,000 per month. In the northeast, the monthly cost can be as high as $15,000 per month. If both the husband and wife require this care, then these numbers double. If only one spouse requires this care, the other spouse needs to have the resources to maintain his or her lifestyle while also paying for the care of the institutionalized spouse. This cost can consume a lifetime of savings and leave the couple devastated—essentially paupers and wards of the state's Medicaid program which will only step in and cover these costs when their assets have been reduced to less than $2,000. Sometimes, Medicaid is confused with the Medicare program which provides health insurance coverage for older Americans. Except in very limited situations, Medicare does not cover the cost of care in a long-term care facility.

The threat of this loss is frightening to most older Americans. Consider how much income a couple would need to have to fund long term care cost without eroding their investment asset base. Self-funding requires a net worth of more than three million dollars in the southern states, and much more in the northeast or California.

This risk can be avoided by planning early. There are solutions that allow individuals and couples to preserve their financial independence and have the confidence there will be assets to leave to their children when they pass. These solutions are very affordable if you get in front of the problem and engage in some advanced planning. Unfortunately, the calls I receive on a daily basis tell us that people do not plan ahead, and they are forced to deal with the problem when the good options no longer exist. For most of our clients, leaving some kind of financial legacy to younger generations, even if the amount is modest, has psychological importance. Not planning for the risk of long-term care will make leaving that financial legacy impossible.

Core Principle Number Two: Save and Invest Systematically

I could fill a library with the financial books written in recent years offering advice on how to develop and maintain a family budget and how to invest your savings. It would be unrealistic to attempt to distill all of that wisdom into a few paragraphs, but at the end of this chapter, I have provided references to the resources I believe give the most solid advice.

There is one piece of advice I do offer with confidence: hire a good financial planner to be your coach and mentor. There is solid data that suggests that individuals and families who use the services of a professional financial advisor will produce better results over time than those who choose to manage their own investment account. One study found that a professional advisor may add as much as three percentage points of value in net portfolio returns, and that's after taxes and fees.

In my experience, there are good advisors who produce more than a three percent advantage. Many of my clients are so fearful of losing what they have, that they keep far too much cash in bank certificates of deposit earning very low interest rates. Because inflation almost always exceeds the CD interest rates, these people are actually losing money.

The greatest value a professional advisor can provide is behavioral coaching. This is particularly important when the markets are turbulent and you are tempted to abandon your asset allocation and move to cash. You may have noticed that you have an urge to sell when the markets are oversold and an urge to buy when the markets are overbought. The Vanguard study I mention looked at a hypothetical investor who was making an investment decision on March 9, 2009—the day the U. S. equity market hit bottom. If that investor had stayed in cash, the value of his investment would have declined 29% by March 2014. An investment in a 100% bond portfolio would have declined 10%. However, a balanced portfolio of 50% equities and 50% bonds would be worth 41% more on that same date, and much more than that in 2018, even after the year-end market decline.

Of course, there are exceptions to every rule. I have clients who have produced astonishing results managing their own portfolio. My observation is that their success usually results from focusing their investments in sectors they know well, likely because they work in or own a business in that sector. But these results are rare, and even when I see them, I realize that, for these clients, investing is something of an obsession that absorbs much of their free time. Most people I know, including myself, are not willing to commit to the time required to get good at investing.

The asset-based fees financial advisors charge to manage your investment account are more reasonable than you think. If you have the right advisor, their fees should be fully aligned with your financial interest. The days when your stockbroker had incentives to churn your account by encouraging you to buy and sell as often as possible are largely gone. Now, most financial advisors charge a fee that is based on the value of your account, so they have an incentive to grow it over time and keep you as a satisfied client.

As I point out elsewhere in this book, the best professional athletes hire personal coaches. Closer to home, I can say that in our law firm, we invest real time and money every year with business coaches, all for the purpose of raising our own game. The reality for most people is that while they think they will create a financial plan and follow it with discipline, without the outside accountability of a financial advisor or coach, almost no one does. If you're seriously pursuing the journey to financial security, hire a coach.

Core Principle Number Three: Be Wary of Debt, and Avoid Consumer Debt Entirely

One of the first pieces of advice your financial advisor will share with you is something I have seen consistently demonstrated by our most successful clients: avoid consumer debt. Using debt in your business or to acquire real estate can make sense and work when managed properly, but you should plan to reduce and eventually eliminate that debt over time.

Consumer debt almost never makes sense. I recall watching a video of Warren Buffett speaking to a group of University of Nebraska students offering financial wisdom and insight. He spent the first several minutes of the speech talking about the dangers of credit card debt. His advice was to avoid them altogether. "Interest rates are very high on credit cards," Buffett said. "Sometimes it's 18 percent. Sometimes it's 20 percent. If I borrowed money at 18 or 20 percent, I'd be broke." I recall my sons receiving unsolicited credit cards with some available balance as they went off to college and thought there was something a bit cynical about a bank sending credit cards to young people who are unprepared for the almost unavoidable temptation to put that card to use.

Talking About Money with the Next Generation

It is still a mystery to me why the educational system we have in the U.S (which many believe is the best in the world) does virtually nothing to prepare young adults to function financially as adults. High school graduates can learn physics, science, language, literature, and world affairs, but we rarely hear about anyone teaching the three core principles I identified earlier. That failure is why a huge percentage of these students are quickly trapped in a cycle of consumer debt from which they are unlikely to escape.

The task of educating the next generation to become financially responsible is left to the family. I believe one of the greatest responsibilities you have as a parent or grandparent is teaching the principles of good financial stewardship to your younger generation family members. Their personal success in life, the success of their marriage, and their physical and emotional health depends on them having established positive behaviors relating to money. There are several great resources available to help you instill these skills, and I have provided a link to our website below with a list of the best ones.

★★★★★★★★★★

Learn more about legendary Texan Dan Duncan, his approach to business and his generosity, particularly with Baylor University Medical Center. The available resources for learning and teaching family members financial stewardship are extensive; my team and I have selected some of the best. We also provide a link to support my position that financial advisors add measurable quantifiable value to the management of your investment portfolio.

www.YourAmericanLegacy.com/resources

YOUR AMERICAN LEGACY

*If you want happiness for a year, inherit
a fortune. If you want happiness for a lifetime,
help someone else.*

—CONFUCIUS

CHAPTER SEVEN

Protect Your Family from the Dark Side of Wealth

The Case of Ethan Couch

Ethan Couch was a sixteen-year-old teenager in June of 2013. He was intoxicated, driving on a restricted license and speeding in a residential area of Burleson, Texas when he lost control of his truck and collided with a group of good Samaritans who had stopped to assist a driver with a disabled SUV. Four people were killed in the collision and a total of nine people were injured. Two passengers in Couch's vehicle suffered serious bodily injury, one with complete paralysis.

Couch was indicted on four counts of manslaughter for recklessly driving under the influence. His attorneys argued that young Ethan didn't know boundaries because his rich parents never gave him any. Ethan suffered from "affluenza," they contended; he needed rehabilitation instead of prison. His defense became known as the "affluenza defense." Ethan was sentenced to ten years of probation and ordered to go through therapy at a long-term in-patient facility. This sentence was viewed by many as incredibly lenient. Ethan's sentence set off what *The New York Times* called "an emotional, angry debate that has stretched far beyond the North Texas suburbs." Two years later, after a viral video surfaced of Ethan violating the terms of his probation playing beer pong, he and his mother ran off to Mexico, prompting an extended manhunt which eventually ended when both of them were captured at a condominium in Puerto Vallarta. Ethan was then sentenced to serve two years in prison.

Having Wealth is More Challenging Than You Think

People who are not wealthy have a hard time imagining there is anything negative about having wealth. You get an entirely different perspective when you hear what the people who have had wealth for some time say. Andrew Carnegie famously said "wealth is an almighty curse." Henry Ford's view was that "fortunes destroy those who inherit them." Alfred Nobel, who established the Nobel Peace Prize was equally skeptical of inherited wealth:

> "I regard large inherited wealth as a misfortune, which merely serves to dull men's faculties. A man who possesses great wealth should, therefore, allow only a small portion to descend to his relatives. Even if he has children, I consider it a mistake to hand over to them considerable sums of money beyond what is necessary for their education. To do so merely encourages laziness and impedes the healthy development of the individual's capacity to make an independent position for himself."

In a now famous *Fortune Magazine* interview in 1986, Warren Buffett expressed his view on leaving wealth to heirs. His personal objective, he said, was to leave his heirs "...so much they could do anything, but not so much they could do nothing."

In today's dollars, Cornelius Vanderbilt would have been worth more than $200 billion. That's more than the net worth of Warren Buffett and Bill Gates combined. Cornelius Vanderbilt endowed my alma mater, Vanderbilt University, in 1873. A family reunion at Vanderbilt University in 1973 was attended by 120 members of the Vanderbilt family. Not one of them was even a millionaire.

A member of the Rothschild family reportedly said this: "It requires a great deal of boldness and a great deal of caution to make a great fortune; and when you have got it, it requires ten times as much wit to keep it."

While I believe financial success is generally a good thing, there is no question there is a dark side to it. We have to recognize and plan for that dark side because the consequences of not doing so can be very destructive. Every estate planner can recite stories of inheritances that were quickly wasted by heirs, sometimes by making poor investments, but other times by spending it on cars, boats, drugs, or alcohol. An Ohio State University study funded by the Bureau of Labor Statistics found that one third of people who received an inheritance had negative savings within two years of receiving the inheritance. A lifetime of work, struggle, and saving by the senior generation—dissipated in less than two years. That heir is actually worse off than they would have been had they received nothing from the parent because they are not only impoverished, but they now have to live with the sting of their personal foolishness.

What the Heirs Say

You also get an interesting perspective on inherited wealth when you talk to children and grandchildren who grew up in wealthy families. To be sure, none of these people want to give up the security of their financial position, but they are very often conflicted by it. William Vanderbilt, the grandson of Cornelius, reportedly remarked that "inherited wealth is a real handicap to happiness... It has left me with nothing to hope for, with nothing definite to seek or strive for."

Terms such as "trust fund baby" and "affluenza" have worked their way into our common vocabulary for a reason. Books have been written about this, and the concerns you hear expressed are painful. Children from wealth fear they cannot trust the friendships they have because they are not totally sure if they are experiencing a genuine personal relationship or if their friends like being around the things their money buys. Even worse, they may fear their friends are not really their friends, but instead are people working to manipulate them and separate them from their money.

Adult children who come from wealth also have a real insecurity about just how well they would function in the world but for the resources provided by their parents. They know there's a difference between the life they are able to live and the life they would live if they had to make it on their own without the support of family money.

What is an Inheritance Worth?

Most parents would like the confidence of knowing their younger generation family members will possess a work ethic, but they fear that will not be the case. Most of our clients have a deeply-rooted belief that a good work ethic is the very reason their wealth exists, and they express concern that if younger generation family members don't continue to exhibit that behavior, the wealth they inherit will not survive for long.

The temptation to quit working when your inheritance arrives is undeniable. I know that most people have a "number," an amount of income that would allow them to stop working productively and engage in other pursuits. The idea is that one additional dollar earned beyond that "number" just doesn't add any qualitative difference to their life. If an inheritance gets them to that number without working, living the good life from the inheritance is a very seductive option.

I usually do an exercise with my clients to have them understand exactly what they are leaving each of their heirs. I believe an inheritance needs to be viewed in terms of what it will purchase every year over the heir's lifetime, rather than viewed as a dollar amount. If the projected inheritance of an heir is, let's say, $2M dollars, what is that really worth to the heir? As I discussed earlier, an inheritance that is properly invested and managed over time should allow the beneficiary to take 4% to 5% of the value of that account every year while allowing the asset base to continue to grow over time at 6% to 7% so that the annual consumable cash flow is protected from inflation. So, if the beneficiary comes into their inheritance at age 40 and they live to age 100, the inheritance received at age 40 would have the same buying power at age 100 as it did the year they received their inheritance. I walked through this exercise recently for a client who wanted to leave each of his children $3M dollars when he and his wife passed. I did the math for him and pointed out that this inheritance would be worth $120,000 to $150,000 of additional income to each of their children each year. The client's reaction was immediate and almost violent! "Oh my," he said, "If they had that available, they'd quit working. I can never let that happen!"

Hope is Not a Strategy

It is very common for us to work with parents of children who have disappointed them with their lack of financial maturity, failed marriages, or drug or alcohol abuse. When I see this, and I do see it often, I hear parents react in one of two ways. They may first choose to do nothing to protect those children or grandchildren because they hope they will eventually change. It's difficult to be the bearer of bad news, but more than thirty years of working with families has taught me that, while transformation does sometimes happen, most adults will continue to behave the way they are behaving now. If they have reached their late 20s or 30s, it is unlikely the behavior patterns, particularly those relating to money, will ever change. I encourage clients to face up to that reality and deal with it.

The other reaction I hear, almost as frequently as the first, is to simply say "let's cut them out entirely" or "they made their bed, now they can sleep in it." This is driven from a combination of anger and disappointment. I find myself encouraging these clients to look at these potential heirs differently. "Do you still love them?" I ask. Usually the answer is a grudging "yes." "Do you want them living under a bridge when they're seventy years old and you're gone and can't rescue them?" The reaction to that takes longer, but usually it's "no." There are far better solutions available than leaving an inheritance with no planning and the harsh alternative of cutting them out entirely.

There are Good Solutions

Most of our clients brighten up when they learn there are several solutions that can protect heirs from their worst instincts without continuing to enable them. Most of the time I spend in client meetings is spent teaching my clients how these solutions work.

It is very common for us to recommend leaving an heir's inheritance in a discretionary trust for the beneficiary while giving the trustee of that trust broad authority to distribute or withhold funds based on the heir's provable financial needs and conduct. This is a common solution today in the United States, and one I recommend often in my practice. In many cases, however, I enhance that solution in ways that encourages the heir to work, to consider entrepreneurial opportunities, and to explore charitable passions. I have designed incentive trusts that provide distributions will be made to the beneficiary only if he or she becomes productively employed and produces a W-2 for the trustee each year. In that model, the beneficiary is required to make a certain amount of earned income as a precondition to receiving any distribution from the trust. But if the beneficiary was successful enough to do that, the trustee could match the amount of earned income by distributing some multiple of the excess over that earned income as an incentive to stimulate the beneficiary's ambition. The incentive trusts I have drafted have all had exceptions carved out in case the beneficiary had a genuine health impairment or decided to pursue a worthwhile career that did not pay well.

I have designed trusts that have earmarked funds specifically for investment in business opportunities, but only after a serious business plan was put forward by the beneficiary. I have also provided for the distribution of "practice money" to beneficiaries to give them the opportunity to invest and make mistakes, and to hopefully build self-confidence and self-esteem by having the experience that not everything has been simply handed to them.

There is an overlap between financial and legal solutions, and that is why it is so important for the client's estate planning attorney and the client's financial advisor to work closely together. If they don't, there is a very real risk the solutions will not be coordinated and will not work as they were intended to work. I discuss additional planning strategies in the next chapters where I focus on legal strategies and solutions.

★★★★★★★★★★

Learn more about the sad case of Ethan Couch and the "Affluenza" defense. I also provide a link to some other resources that underscore the challenge of having wealth and protecting younger generation family members from its harmful effects. A link to the Ohio State University research supports my proposition that one-third of inheritors spend their entire inheritance in less than two years if it is left to them without the protection of a trust.

www.YourAmericanLegacy.com/resources

YOUR AMERICAN LEGACY

"It's good to have money and the things that
money can buy, but it's good, too, to check up once
in a while and make sure that you haven't lost the
things that money can't buy"

—GEORGE LORIMER

PART 2

The Second Building Block:
Protect Your Financial Legacy
for Generations

There are real risks that threaten to destroy what you have built and saved. Some of those come from the outside and include things like the court system, taxes, lawsuits, divorce, and bankruptcy. Risks to your financial security also come from the inside and can be threatened by things like financial immaturity and substance abuse. It can take a very long time to recreate wealth that's been lost. But it doesn't have to happen—the tools available today to protect you and your family are more powerful than at any other time in history. We take a look at those tools in the next three chapters.

Thinking well is wise;
Planning well; wiser;
Doing well wisest and best of all

– Persian Proverb

THE LEGACY
PLANNING
PYRAMID™

YOUR AMERICAN LEGACY

"Death is not the end. There remains the litigation
over the estate"

—AMBROSE BIERCE

CHAPTER EIGHT

Train Wrecks and How to Avoid Them

Not Having a Plan Has Consequences

Prince died in April of 2016 with an estate estimated at $300 million. He was 57 years old and had no estate plan. Nothing. A Minnesota judge had to decide how to distribute Prince's estate among his six siblings, but the court case became complicated when other potential heirs surfaced, including an inmate in a federal prison claiming to be Prince's son.

Everyone knows they need an estate plan. We have all heard the horror stories that result from failing to have one. There are books and websites that recount the disastrous consequences of not having one, including the names of well-known Americans who should have known better. Abraham Lincoln died without a will and it took two years for his estate to be settled. Fortunately, a sympathetic Congress made sure his wife and children were provided for in the interim.

Singer Whitney Houston had a will when she drowned in her bathtub in February 2012. It was signed in 1993, one month before her daughter was born. She never reviewed it, and apparently never considered whether her daughter was emotionally mature enough to receive an unrestricted inheritance. The daughter, Bobbi Kristina Brown, was eighteen when her mother died. According to the terms of the will, she was to receive $2 million when she turned twenty-one and the balance of her mother's estate sometime later. Bobbi Kristina turned twenty-one, got the $2 million and died shortly thereafter as a result of drowning and drug intoxication.

Football fans will recognize the name Joe Robbie. He was the founder of the Miami Dolphins, and the stadium where the Dolphins played bore his name. He passed away in 1990, and his family was forced to sell the Dolphins franchise to pay a reported $47 million in estate taxes. Proper planning could have prevented that. Olympic gold medalist Florence Griffith Joyner had a will when she died, but no one knew where she kept it, and that spawned a probate court battle that took four years to resolve.

In our office, we call these failures "train wrecks." They happen in slow motion and they are gut-wrenching to watch.

What You Lose by Not Planning

The motivation to put a legal plan in place increases when you fully understand what you lose when you do not plan.

Which of These Motivate You to Plan?

Probate Court. Without a plan, you put yourself and your property in the hands of a probate court judge. This is true if you become incapacitated. This is also true when you die. The probate process takes months or years, and opens your private business affairs to public inspection and significantly increases legal fees and court costs. Most people think they avoid this outcome by having their will made. That is not true. As we discuss later, a will usually guarantees probate. However, the probate process is entirely avoidable.

Next Spouse Protection. Without a plan, you lose the opportunity to protect your assets from your spouse's next spouse. It is common for spouses to remarry after one spouse dies. This is especially true for a husband who loses his wife. When this happens, the estate the couple created together is at risk to the influence as well as the legal rights of the new spouse. This is an important issue for about half of the married clients I see in my practice. The level of concern increases significantly with those clients who have had a family member lose an inheritance because of a late in life second marriage of a relative. My experience is that these outcomes are not always the result of malicious or greedy intentions; more often, they are the result of inattention to the way assets are titled. There are excellent trust solutions that balance the need to provide financial support for a surviving spouse while at the same time ensuring the next generation will receive an inheritance that should legitimately pass to them. However, this is a sleeper issue and it's almost never a matter of discussion until I bring it up.

Divorce, Lawsuit, and Bankruptcy Protection for Heirs. Without a plan, you lose the opportunity to provide your beneficiaries with lifetime protection from divorce and judgment creditors. This kind of protection can be provided to your beneficiaries while also allowing them to retain personal control over the investment of their inheritance as well as control over distributions to themselves and their children.

Protection from Immaturity or Lack of Financial Skill. Not every heir has the maturity or skill to manage an inheritance. Without a plan, you lose the opportunity to provide heirs who lack that maturity or skill with a structure that will ensure their inheritance will be invested wisely and continue to provide financial security into their old age. The need for this kind of help will always be required when the beneficiaries are minors, but the need for this kind of protection is also common with adult children and surviving spouses as well.

Protection from Your Own Judgment Creditors. Your assets are generally available to satisfy judgments from people that sue you. While you cannot protect yourself from creditors you choose—such as the bank that loans you money—you can protect yourself from judgments obtained by what we call involuntary creditors. With litigation becoming more common, particularly against professionals and business owners, this kind of protection can provide real peace of mind should an action be brought against you. To some extent, anyone who drives a car or engages in any kind of activity that creates a risk of causing damage to others needs this protection. The tools to provide this protection are there, but you have to use them.

The Cost of Long-Term Care. Without a plan, you lose the opportunity to keep your financial assets from being consumed to pay your nursing home bill or home health care costs. There are some very powerful solutions available that can provide this protection, but to work most effectively, they need to be deployed well in advance of your need for care.

Income & Capital Gains Tax. If you fail to plan, you may lose the opportunity to legally reduce or eliminate federal and state income tax and capital gains taxes. The solutions that can provide this protection are not well known, but when properly deployed, they can dramatically reduce the tax you or your family would otherwise be required to pay.

The Estate Tax. As Joe Robbie's family discovered, without the right plan in place, you lose the opportunity to reduce or eliminate the federal estate tax. While the federal estate tax exemption has increased significantly in recent years, the number of states that have adopted some form of transfer tax upon death has increased. Most of those states have exemptions that are much lower than the federal exemption. However, with proper planning, both the federal and state estate taxes can be reduced or eliminated entirely. Unless you are mega-rich, the estate tax is a voluntary tax.

Forced Division of Hard-to-Divide Assets. When you fail to plan, you may force the division of a farm or family business that has been built over generations. As I discuss later, the division of these kinds of assets can be destructive and may not even be possible without liquidating the asset. Proper planning can protect these assets for generations.

Deciding Who Will Raise Your Children. If you have minor children, you probably go out to dinner occasionally and leave the children with a babysitter. The instructions you leave for that four hours away are often far more extensive than the instructions you currently have in place if you went away permanently. When you don't plan, you lose the opportunity to decide who will have custody of your minor children if you become incapacitated or die. If you don't plan for this, the decision will be left up to a judge who doesn't know your children or any of the contenders for the guardian role. You also lose the opportunity to provide the decision-making guidelines you would want your children's new parents to follow. If you don't have minor children, you probably know someone who does. Mention this to them.

Choosing Who Will Make Your Health Care Choices. When you don't plan, you lose the opportunity to choose who will make healthcare choices for you if you can't make them yourself. The laws of your state will provide a list of persons who have the authority to make those decisions for you, but the individuals your state legislature chooses may not be the same as those you would choose. The individuals you would want making those decisions will not even have the ability to discuss your condition with your doctor if they are not listed on a properly executed HIPPA (Health Insurance Portability and Accountability Act) form.

Train Wrecks Do Not Have to Happen

None of these things have to happen. You and your family do not have to be the victim of a train wreck. These wrecks are entirely preventable.

★★★★★★★★★★

In the resource links to this chapter, I have provided links to several websites that include stories of estate planning train wrecks of famous people who died without proper planning. We have included books and articles on this topic as well.

www.YourAmericanLegacy.com/resources

YOUR AMERICAN LEGACY

"The fear of death follows from the fear of life. A man who lives fully is prepared to die at any time."

—Mark Twain

CHAPTER NINE

Overcoming the Planning Phobia

Lincoln had a War to Run. You Don't.

President Lincoln was busy managing a civil war, so we might understand his failure to make a will. But most of us don't have distractions of that magnitude. Even though we all know we should have an estate plan, less than half of American adults have gone to the trouble to make a simple will. Even fewer have had their plan reviewed in the last ten years.

Most of us are realistic enough to know that we could become incapacitated and that we will die someday. So, why is it that we are so reluctant to plan for what we know is certain to happen? My answer to that question is that people see the experience of creating an estate plan as the legal equivalent of being forced to eat vegetables they don't like. Confronting your own mortality can be unsettling, so it's easy to give in to the temptation of dealing with the here-and-now issues and procrastinate on planning for our eventual incapacity and death.

If you are serious about creating a legacy that has a positive impact on the generations to come, it is critical that you provide a legal roadmap for the orderly management and transfer of your financial wealth. That roadmap can ensure that your financial legacy will be appropriately managed and not cause harm to the family members who are too immature to use it wisely. It can also ensure that the assets you have worked a lifetime to accumulate will not be lost by an heir who has a failed marriage, a judgment creditor or business failure. It will prevent the risk of permanent fractures in family relationships. It can ensure that the younger generation family members will have a real measure of lifetime financial security and personal freedom. A thoughtful, well-crafted estate plan is an essential building block of your legacy.

Three Key Fears

Most people dread the thought of sitting in a room with a lawyer discussing how their assets should be managed and distributed if they become incapacitated or die. Let's take a look at the fears behind the reluctance to create a basic estate plan. From my experience, this reluctance is fueled by three fundamental fears. Let's embrace those fears and deal with them right now.

Fear Number One: Losing Control

This is the most common fear, and it's always caused by a lack of understanding about how modern estate planning tools work. I constantly have to remind our clients that most of the planning tools used today leaves the client in total control—and this includes the power to manage and invest their assets and, in most cases, the power to spend the assets as they choose while they are living. Some advanced estate tax planning solutions do require giving up some control, but recent legislation in several states allowing for the creation of self-settled trusts and the use of trust protectors has softened that loss of control to a level that almost all of my clients find acceptable once they understand how those solutions work. Solutions that position you to qualify for Medicaid and Veterans Administration benefits that pay for long term care also require some relinquishment of direct control, but some new, innovative tools do allow for the retention of a significant measure of control over the management of the assets as well as control over the recipients of those assets at death. My bottom line is this: the fear of losing control over your assets should not be a reason to put off planning.

Fear Number Two:
The Intimidation of Legal Jargon

It has happened dozens of times in my office—clients drop a copy of their estate planning documents on my desk and then say something like: "Here is my estate plan. We signed all this, but we have no idea what it says." Clients have a fear of being intimidated by a lawyer sitting behind a large desk with a wall full of impressive diplomas speaking a language they don't understand. It is very uncomfortable to feel pushed into signing a large stack of legal documents when you are not clear on how those documents work. I agree with that sentiment.

I also want to be realistic. Unless you want to enroll in a post-graduate law school program on estate planning, you will probably never fully understand every provision in your estate planning documents. A thorough, well-prepared set of estate planning documents contain a lot of information. Most of it is there to provide clear answers to situations that rarely occur. But because unusual things can happen, good estate planners include these provisions in your documents.

What I say here will be heresy to some lawyers, but I will say it anyway: I do not think it is necessary to fully absorb all the technical fine print in those documents before you sign them. I look at these provisions in the same way I look at the fuel injection system in my car—I want to know how my car works, but I don't have to understand how fuel is metered into the cylinders. It is not difficult to reach a comfortable level of understanding of the issues in your estate plan that actually matter to you. In my experience with several thousand clients, there are only three:

Who is in Control? You should know who is in control of your estate plan at every stage. Generally, the person in control will be you while you are living and competent. But you will also want to know who will take over and manage your assets and who will make health care choices for you if you are not capable of doing it yourself. If you are married, you'll want to know who will be in control after you're gone but while your spouse is still living and competent. You will also want to know who will be in control after your spouse is no longer alive or competent. You will want to know who will manage the inheritance your heirs receive. You may have an answer if you should die fairly soon, when your children are teenagers, for example—but that answer may be different if your children are older. Decisions about the succession of control require some thought. You may need to consider having a non-family member or a corporate trustee fulfill that role. You may choose to create a team of two or three individuals or an individual and a corporate trustee. This issue is also the most frequent source of amendments to estate plans because the people we choose to fill these roles sometimes move away, become ill, or die.

Who receives what? Most of us have a good idea about who we want to leave our assets to when we die, so understanding this part of your plan should be easy. However, a proper plan has to address an alternative disposition of assets because beneficiaries sometimes die before you do. You also need to consider who will receive your tangible personal property or heirloom items. I discuss this more in Chapter Thirteen, but I've mentioned it here because these are the items that create the most conflict in families. If you have charities that are important to you, you may want to consider including them in your plan. I have found that our clients who have been consistently charitable during their lives often fail to consider including their favorite charities in their estate plan, and that is usually an oversight because the estate planner didn't ask about it.

How and when your heirs receive their inheritance. This element of your estate plan is not quite as obvious as who receives what. However, this is where good estate planners truly add value. Most people, if they don't know the options that are available to them, will provide for a simple outright distribution of an inheritance to a beneficiary. In my experience, this is almost always the least desirable option. Leaving assets in trust is almost always a better solution, and it is much easier than most people think.

Creating trusts for heirs can provide a very significant level of protection for them in the event they go through a divorce or are involved in a lawsuit that results in a judgment creditor. It is possible to provide divorce and lawsuit protection for the heir while also allowing the heir to control their own trust. However, giving an heir control over their trust is not always a good idea. If you have an heir that is financially immature, vulnerable to the negative influence of a spouse or unscrupulous friends or has a drug or alcohol issue, there are solid trust solutions that can provide lifetime protection and financial security for that heir.

If you are concerned that an inheritance might destroy your heir's work ethic, I mentioned in a previous chapter how a trust can be drafted to create incentives to work as a condition to receiving benefits from the trust. If the beneficiary has special needs that entitle them to benefits under your state's Medicaid or MediCal program, those issues will drive the design of the trust for that heir. Our clients are almost always surprised—in a good way—about the power and flexibility of the planning tools that are available to them.

These three essential elements of your estate plan can be absorbed fairly quickly if you work with an estate planner who is genuinely interested in having you confidently understand your plan. In our practice, each of these three elements is clearly presented in a one or two-page flow chart that becomes the reference for your overall plan. I believe you should understand your plan well enough that you could draw it on a napkin for friends if you had the desire to explain it to them. It is the estate planner's task to get you to that level of confidence using your language, not lawyer language.

It can be done; in fact, it's done all the time now. The professional estate planning community is getting the message that it is no longer acceptable to expect clients to sign legal documents based on a lawyer's superior knowledge. The curtain is being pulled back in a lot of professions as more information becomes available online. Consumers are now more empowered than ever to take greater ownership in understanding the professional services they consume. This is a good thing.

Fear Number Three: Not knowing the financial investment required to create the plan.

Most people have no idea what kind of financial or time investment is required to create an estate plan that accomplishes their goals. The fear of committing to an estate planning process without knowing the investment required to complete it properly is entirely legitimate. However, that concern is one that can be easily addressed before beginning the process.

While hourly billing continues to be the prevailing approach to setting fees in large law firms, most estate planning firms, including my own, work on a fixed fee basis for most engagements. In this kind of arrangement, you will know the financial investment required before you engage the attorney to do the work for you, and that fee is generally not affected by phone calls, emails or additional time spent answering your questions. When I practiced using the old hourly fee model, I found that clients wanted to talk fast and tell me only what they thought I needed to know. When I shifted to the fixed fee model, I found that I could spend time getting to know the client, look at pictures of their grandchildren, and hear about their recent vacation. My clients don't appreciate how valuable these informal conversations are in helping me gain the personal insights I need to develop an estate plan that is customized to meet their unique needs.

I hope you can see now that failing to plan will almost always guarantee a disaster with consequences that can last for several generations. I also hope you can see that the fears that are keeping you from taking action to prevent those disasters can be easily addressed.

Proper planning is not just something you do to avoid train wrecks. I would like for you to think bigger about the process. I would like for you to see it as something that adds meaning and clarity to your life in a profoundly positive way. I will expand on that idea in later chapters of this book.

There are No Good Excuses

There are no good reasons for not having a basic estate plan in place regardless of how young and healthy you are. It is a fundamental responsibility as adults to not leave a mess for your family to clean up. In most cases, a basic estate plan can be thoughtfully designed, drafted, and signed in less than thirty days. If you haven't taken this step, do it now. Life is uncertain.

★★★★★★★★★★

I'm not the first to point out that people look for reasons to procrastinate when it comes to getting their affairs in order. The books in the resource link to this chapter will help you move past a fear of the planning process.

www.YourAmericanLegacy.com/resources

YOUR AMERICAN LEGACY

"You cannot multiply wealth by dividing it."

—ADRIAN ROGERS

CHAPTER TEN

Rethinking the "Divide and Distribute" Mindset

What Building Wealth and Nuclear Physics Have in Common

Years ago, early in my legal career, an elderly and financially successful client took the opportunity to share some wisdom with me. The name of this gentleman has long since faded into the mist of time, but I recall quite clearly the insight he offered. "Stan, let me tell you this," he said. "If a man starts out in business with absolutely nothing—zero—and starts to build his net worth, growing that net worth from zero to $100,000 is almost impossible." He continued: "But if that man is somehow able to defy the odds and build his net worth to $100,000, then growing it to $1 million is merely difficult."

That made sense to me, but the surprising twist to this teaching moment came when he said, "If that man is able to somehow work his net worth up to $1 million, then growing the next $20 million is inevitable." His insight was new for me at the time, but as I reflect on it now, several decades later, I know from my experience in working with thousands of clients that he was exactly right.

Wealth behaves like uranium used in building a nuclear generator. Small amounts of it are just useless, inert material, but when larger amounts of it are assembled, and a critical mass is reached, the material becomes amazingly powerful. That power is destroyed when it is diffused.

I have reflected often on my mentor's advice in my work with clients. My observation of this phenomenon has ripened into a kind of axiom about wealth that has proven to be largely true in my experience:

The Law of Division:

"Wealth that is divided and distributed is quickly dissipated;
Wealth that is aggregated and managed inevitably grows."

This concept has not been widely adopted yet. The most common estate distribution technique is to divide and distribute wealth. I call this the "Divide and Distribute" mentality. I see "divide and distribute" thinking expressed in almost every will or living trust I review. This "divide and distribute" mentality is traditionally how estate planning has been approached by almost everyone, including the lawyers who are in this line of work. I want to make the case in this chapter that there is a different and more empowering way to think about planning your estate.

Shirtsleeves to Shirtsleeves in Three Generations

The "Divide and Distribute" concept explains an observation most often expressed in the old proverb "shirtsleeves to shirtsleeves in three generations." The concept embedded in this expression is universally recognized. The Scottish say, "The father buys, the son builds, the grandchild sells, and his son begs." In Japan, the expression is, "Rice paddies to rice paddies in three generations." In China, there's another variation: "Wealth never survives three generations." The idea that wealth is created and then destroyed in three generations is not just a quaint cultural expression. A 1987 study published by J.L. Ward, a professor at

Northwestern University's Kellogg School of Management, found that only 20% of family businesses make it to the third generation and just 13% last through that generation. Ancient expressions like these, especially when validated by solid research and our own experience, command our attention and cause us to ask: "Is this outcome inevitable? Or are there strategies we can install that will prevent the inevitable dissipation of our life's work?" I think there are—in fact, I'm sure of it.

What an Irish Pub and an Italian Gun maker can Teach Us

In 2008, the Bank of South Korea published the results of a research project that studied the world's oldest businesses and discovered that there were more than five thousand businesses in the world over two hundred years old. Several of these businesses have been around for much longer. Sean's Bar, a thriving Irish pub in a small town in central Ireland, was founded in 900 A.D. The Italian gun manufacturer Beretta was founded in 1526. The study also identified a family owned business in Japan—a construction company specializing in building temples—that had been owned and operated by the same family for over fourteen hundred years when it was acquired by a larger construction company in 2006. The United States is a young country, and not many of the world's oldest businesses are located here. But there are several farms, plantations, and businesses in the U.S. that are thriving and date back to the 1600s. Some of them are still operated by the founding families. So it can be done.

The Secret to Longevity

The most common directive clients give an estate planner when they are making their will or trust is the instruction to "divide and distribute" the assets. If dividing and distributing assets inevitably leads to their dissipation, isn't is worth considering alternatives to that model? I believe the secret to the long-term survival of a farm or business—or even a portfolio of marketable securities—is structuring ownership of the asset so that division and distribution is not required when the asset owner dies. There are more legal tools to accomplish that result available today than at any other time in history. These options usually include the use of some form of irrevocable trust owning limited partnership or limited liability company interests. None of the options require the senior generation to give up control over management and the best solutions also allow the senior generation to continue to enjoy the economic benefit of the asset base as long as they live.

However, a legal structure alone is not sufficient. I am convinced the multi-generational viability of a farm or business requires an emotional connection with the history and values of the enterprise that goes deeper than a mere a financial interest. You see the kind of emotional connection I'm talking about demonstrated by Joan Appleton. She was the ninth generation owner of Appleton Farm in Ipswich, Massachusetts which was established in 1636. Joan had no heirs, so rather than selling the farm to developers for tens of millions of dollars, she kept the farm until she died and left it to a charitable land trust that is required to maintain the property as a working farm open to the community forever. You get that same sense of passion from Atkins & Pearce, a textile manufacturer founded in 1817 in Kentucky which is still owned by the same family. That kind of passion is not automatically transferred to younger generations. It is shared daily by senior generation family members who understand the value the farm or business brings to the community and to its employees. I will explore some strategies that can build that deeper connection in the later chapters of this book.

Longevity requires preparing younger generation family members for the leadership role they will play as the enterprise is transitioned to the next generation. Justin Miller, an attorney and strategic wealth advisor at BNY Mellon underscores the need for families to proactively focus on creating a structure and process for family governance. He points out that there are a number of effective models for family governance. In the United States, we are familiar with the representative model of governance in a political context. That same concept is frequently adapted as a family governance model. Miller makes the point that the representative model is usually not a pure democracy. Family members choose representatives, and by established family rules, the representatives chosen may be required to be individuals that have satisfied certain requirements, such as a college education or some kind of professional training. However, every family member is a beneficiary of the family enterprise. Pro-active family governance is an important process. And it is a process, not a one-time event. That is why I encourage our clients to take advantage of coaching programs such as those offered by the Institute for Preparing Heirs and the Aspen Family Business Group.

The King Ranch Story

In the late 1800s and early 1900s, most Texas ranchers adopted "divide and distribute" thinking when they made their wills. This resulted in large ranches becoming smaller ranches as each generation died off. The Kleberg family owned one of the largest ranches in the U.S. In 1935, the Kleberg's made the decision to do something that was, even by today's standards, rather innovative. They formed a corporation and transferred the ranch property to the corporation. As a consequence, when a shareholder died, there was no need to divide anything other than shares in the corporation. Today, shares in the King Ranch Corporation are owned by several dozen family members. By maintaining the ranch as a unified enterprise, it continues to be one of the largest in the country—it's actually larger than the State of Rhode Island. The corporation also operates a ranch store where you can purchase ranch branded clothing items, and it generates additional cash by licensing the King Ranch brand to Ford Motor Company. A professional manager who is not a family member now runs the corporation, but the family continues to benefit from the decision made over eighty years ago by their ancestors to not adopt the "divide and distribute" model.

To Divide or Not to Divide

Sometimes it does make sense to divide things. We would not want children who can't get along to be forced to do business with each other. We also may not want to force younger family members to maintain an asset just because the older generation wanted to perpetuate an unrealistic fantasy that their life's work will continue on forever. However, it is my experience that families are too reflexive in their willingness to divide and distribute assets. I encourage them to at least consider the possibility of the don't-divide option before they choose to divide things up.

We are often able to create structures that allow assets to be maintained and managed over multiple generations by establishing a system of governance that allows the family to function democratically in determining how the enterprise will be managed over time. That structure can also set the ground rules for how the family can choose to terminate the structure and divide or sell the assets if conflict makes the continuation of the enterprise problematic.

The concept of not dividing things should be seriously explored before any decision is made to "divide and distribute" family wealth.

★★★★★★★★★★★

I provide a link to the research generated by the Bank of South Korea study in 2008 that I mention in this chapter. I have also provided links to two coaching programs I know to be useful in helping prepare heirs for family business responsibility. You will also find a link to the legendary King Ranch; it is just one of many examples I could have provided to illustrate the point that properly managing—and not dividing assets at death can produce powerful results for generations of family members.

www.YourAmericanLegacy.com/resources

YOUR AMERICAN LEGACY

"The length of this document defends it well against the risk of its being read."

—Winston Churchill

CHAPTER ELEVEN

Create a Plan that Works

Hollywood Actually Made This Ancient Law Interesting

In the 2011 movie *The Descendants*, George Clooney played the role of an attorney who was also the trustee of a family trust created by his family back in the 1800's. The trust owned a large tract of land on the island of Kauai. The land was worth millions to developers, but was also a family legacy. The trust was expiring because a law called the Rule Against Perpetuities was forcing the trust to terminate, thus prompting the family drama surrounding the issue of whether to sell the land or preserve it. If someone had bet me in law school that someone would make a movie about the Rule Against Perpetuities and actually make it interesting, I would have taken that bet. Almost anyone who has been to law school would agree that a movie having anything to do with this arcane law, crafted in medieval England and brought over to the colonies by the early settlers, would surely put any audience to sleep.

Distilled simply, this ancient law, which was eventually adopted in some form by every state, prevents a trust from lasting more than a certain period of time, usually about 120 years. But things have changed. In the last few years, many states have extended the length of time property can be held in trust—in some cases for as long as 365 years. A few states eliminated the rule entirely which allows a trust created today to last forever. If the ancestors of George Clooney's character had been planning their estate under the law that exists today, the trust would not be required to terminate, the family drama would have been avoided and there would have been no movie.

Planning Tools Are More Powerful Than Ever

In the last twenty years, the developments in trust law have created planning tools that are more powerful and more flexible than at any time in U.S. history. The ability to create trusts that last forever is just one example. Another recent development allows you to create a trust, make yourself the beneficiary, and still have the assets in that trust be protected from your future creditors and the estate tax. This allows you to shift the future growth on your business or investment accounts so that all of the future growth is outside the federal and state estate tax systems—and you can continue to be a beneficiary of that trust. This kind of planning was not possible even twenty-five years ago.

Another example: back in the day, when you created an irrevocable trust, it was very clear you were locked into the terms of the trust and couldn't change it. That is not quite true today. Most states now provide a statutory procedure for modifying irrevocable trusts if all the stakeholders agree. But even without that agreement, changes can be made by a trust protector. The trust protector concept has long been accepted in offshore trusts, but has only recently become commonplace in trusts created domestically. A trust protector is a person you know and trust who is given the right to make significant modifications to the trust. These changes can be made while you are living, but the trust protector can continue to exercise the power to modify your trust long after you are gone to make certain the trust continues to accomplish your original intentions.

The law also permits you to retain the right to remove the trustee of your irrevocable trust as long as you select a new trustee who is not your relative or your employee.

What About the Estate Tax and the Inheritance Tax?

The federal estate tax—or the "death tax" as politicians call it—was once the primary factor that motivated individuals to create an estate plan. Today, there is still an estate tax, but the exemptions are far larger than they have ever been before, so only a very small percentage of American families are currently impacted by that tax. In 2019, it is possible for an individual to transfer—during life or upon death—$11,400,000 free of any federal transfer tax burden. A married couple can transfer double that amount. That amount will be cut in half in 2026, at least as the law is currently written, so it is important to consider the impact of that future reduction in the exemption as you plan. For most individuals and couples, the federal estate tax is no longer an issue.

Even if your estate is large enough to have estate tax exposure, there are planning tools that can be deployed to eliminate the federal estate tax on the first $40 million dollars or more of wealth. The use of entities such as limited liability companies coupled with a gift and sale of assets to some version of a self-settled irrevocable trust can produce these very powerful results. This is just one example. There are a number of very powerful estate tax saving tools, and most of them can be deployed without requiring the senior generation to give up investment control of the asset base.

Seventeen states have adopted a separate estate tax or inheritance tax system that applies to residents of those states. New York City has a separate city estate tax. The inheritance tax is a bit different than the estate tax. The estate tax is assessed at the estate level and paid before distributions are made to the beneficiaries. The inheritance tax is assessed at the beneficiary level, and the rate generally varies depending on the relationship of the beneficiary to the person who passed. For example, a child heir may be taxed on the inheritance he or she receives at a very low rate or pay no tax at all on his or her inheritance. However, a cousin who inherits property from an uncle may pay tax at a much higher rate. With proper planning, it is now possible for you to protect the assets you have built and saved from both the federal, state and local estate and inheritance taxes for generations in ways that an English land baron could not imagine.

The Basics Should Come First

Before you become too caught up in these amazing new estate planning power tools, you should first implement a basic foundational estate plan. I recommend that you get this done in the event something happens to you before you get around to doing more comprehensive planning. For most American families, a basic estate plan is the only estate plan you will need.

What Should a Basic Estate Plan Include?

I will be upfront about my personal bias—I recommend that a revocable living trust be used as the foundational estate-planning document for almost every individual and married couple unless qualification for government benefits to pay for long term care is an important planning objective. There are situations in which a will-based plan is an appropriate choice, but I believe a revocable living trust is the best solution for most people. A basic revocable living trust plan includes several planning documents that go beyond the living trust document itself. Generally, a foundational estate plan should include:

> **A Revocable Living Trust.** The revocable living trust is an individual trust if you are unmarried. If you are married, you may have one joint trust or two separate trusts depending on your situation. A living trust or trusts, when properly funded, prevents the need for a court-supervised guardianship if you become incapacitated, and also prevents a probate proceeding when you die. A living trust allows you to get your affairs in order so that your estate matters can be quickly and efficiently settled. As valuable as this benefit is, it is even more valuable if you own property in more than one state. A trust can eliminate the need for a court supervised probate proceeding in all of the states where property is owned. I

do need to underscore the importance of coordinating the changes in ownership and beneficiary designations with your trust plan. A trust, by itself, does not avoid probate. Your assets have to be properly transferred to the trust for the trust to work properly. This is called "funding" your trust, and it is an essential—and often overlooked—component of creating a revocable living trust estate plan.

A General Durable Power of Attorney. There are certain assets [such as IRA and 401(k) accounts] that should not be transferred to your living trust. There is a separate strategy that coordinates the transfer of these assets at your death with your living trust plan. However, the general durable power of attorney is necessary to provide for the management of these assets held in your individual name while you are living in the event you become incapacitated.

Health Care Decision Documents. A health care power of attorney allows you name the sequence of persons who can make health care and end of life decisions for you. This should be accompanied by a HIPPA form naming all the individuals who you want to have access to your medical information (even if they don't have any decision-making authority), and a living will that expresses your end-of-life intentions in the event you're not competent to participate in that decision.

A Pour-Over Will. If assets are discovered that were never titled into your revocable living trust, this document will ensure they are distributed under the terms of the trust. The assets passing under your pour-over will go through the probate process, but at least they end up where you want them to go. If your trust owns all of your assets, the pour over will generally does not need to be admitted to probate. I explain the pour over will as a kind of "air bag" similar to the one our clients have in their automobiles. We want our air bag to be there and function if we need it, but we would prefer that it never deploy. The same is true for our pour-over will.

Name Guardians of Your Minor Children. If you have minor children, your plan should include a nomination of a testamentary guardian for your children and a back-up guardian in case the guardian you name cannot serve. This is usually done in your will, but it can also be done in a power of attorney document.

Your estate plan does not have to be a boring document crafted in legalese. I encourage our clients to think aspirationally about the guidance they want to provide to their trustees. This includes instructions the trustees can refer to when the time comes to consider distributions to a beneficiary. For example, some clients worry that the availability of funds in a trust may have the effect of reducing a beneficiary's desire to attend college or pursue a purposeful career. This is a legitimate issue. There are many thousands of adults who are beneficiaries of trusts with enough resources to support them in comfort for their entire lives without working. Trustees can be granted a full range of powers to make or withhold distributions if they think the distribution would be harmful to the beneficiary or diminish the beneficiary's work ethic.

The latest technology in drafting estate plans provides a variety of devices that build flexibility into an estate plan to take into account factors the creator of the plan could not have anticipated. My colleague John Warnick, a Denver-based estate planning attorney, founded the Purposeful Planning Institute to teach attorneys and advisors techniques to enhance the planning process with strategies that provide real, practical guidance that goes far beyond the minimum legal requirements. It is very helpful to trustees to understand what was intended when the trust was created, and when the time comes to make—or not make—distributions to a beneficiary. This kind of guidance is essential if the planning is going to be effective in accomplishing its real purpose over a multi-generational time horizon that can span hundreds of years. I discuss some of these tools in greater detail in Chapter Thirteen.

You May Need More Than a Revocable Living Trust

I want to emphasize that a revocable living trust plan does not protect your assets from your own judgment creditors. It also does not protect your assets from being a countable resource under your state's Medicaid programs when you apply for those benefits to pay for the cost of nursing home care. Assets in your revocable living trust are also countable resources if you are seeking to qualify for Veterans Administration Aid and Attendance benefits.

The cost of nursing home care in the U.S. ranges from $5000 per month in some parts of the country to as much as $15,000 per month. Sometimes, both a husband and wife need nursing home care, thereby doubling that cost. Most American families do not have the resources to fund this cost without depleting their life savings. For middle class American families, the cost of long-term care is the single greatest risk to leaving a financial legacy to heirs. A thoughtful analysis of this risk is something that should be a part of the planning process.

If you determine that your income in retirement from all sources would not be adequate to cover this cost, there are solutions you can implement that can protect you and your family from the risk of depleting your life savings and becoming entirely dependent on your state for support. These solutions require more than a revocable living trust. Remember—long-term care solutions work best if they are implemented well in advance of the need for care.

What Your Estate Plan and Your Car Have in Common

My thirty plus years of estate planning experience has taught me one certainty: no estate plan will work the way its creator intended if the plan is not periodically reviewed. I believe that a review should be done annually. You likely have an annual physical and have your car serviced more often than that. Your estate plan deserves the same respect and attention. Many of our clients now come in for annual reviews, and it's surprising to them and to us how many things can get out of order in just one year. Your objective in the annual review is to accomplish three things:

- Confirm that you are still satisfied with your plan, including the individuals or institutions you have selected to play the role of successor trustee, health care agent or guardian of a minor child.

- Confirm that your assets are titled properly and have the proper beneficiary designations.

- Identify any new opportunities that can improve or enhance your plan. Most good estate planners spend real time and money attending continuing education events every year. You will never benefit from any of their new learning unless you give them the opportunity to reconnect with you.

Systematic checkups have been the standard practice in the medical and dental communities for decades. Aviation is far safer today than in years past because the FAA requires an annual diagnostic checkup in order for an airplane to legally be flown. My iPhone is updated several times a year as Apple improves the phone's technology. Systematic annual reviews are now also becoming the standard in the estate planning community. Many of the train wrecks I discuss in Chapter Eight are caused by a failure to review the plan that was created years ago. I believe an annual checklist-driven review of your plan is necessary to preserve the value of your investment in your initial estate plan and to make certain your plan will work the way you want it to work at that point in the future when it's tested.

★★★★★★★★★★

Much misunderstanding surrounds the use of trusts, and much of what I hear from clients is undeservedly negative. Properly designed, trusts can be a powerful multi-generational tool for protecting and preserving wealth and financial security. I have included links to several resources that will provide more information on trusts. One of the resources specifically focuses on the unique planning issues surrounding family vacation cottages.

www.YourAmericanLegacy.com/resources

"Carve your name on hearts, not tombstones. A legacy is etched into the minds of others and the stories they share about you."

– SHANNON L. ALDER

PART 3

The Third Building Block:

Protect the Things That Matter Most

It is gratifying to see the look of relief on the faces of our clients when their estate plan is finally put in place, but the financial security that is protected by an estate plan does not accomplish what is, for many families, the most important objective. Most people want to leave behind solid, well-grounded family members who possess the values that are necessary to live a successful life.

Most people don't consider the possibility that passing these values on is something that can be done on purpose. However, when you begin to develop a thoughtfully imagined legacy plan, you will be challenged to identify the stories, values, and life lessons that are important enough to pass on to younger generations. When you have clarity around the values that matter, you can then create a plan that will create a more satisfying connection with your younger family members, and make it far more likely they will live successful lives, become great parents, and make positive contributions to their communities. This does require some work, but I also know it is a positive, energizing, and empowering experience.

The remaining chapters in this book focus on strategies to help you create your Legacy Plan.

THE LEGACY PLANNING PYRAMID™

LEGACY

FINANCIAL

LEGAL & TAX

YOUR AMERICAN LEGACY

"Your beliefs become your thoughts,
Your thoughts become your words,
Your words become your actions,
Your actions become your habits,
Your habits become your values,
Your values become your destiny."

– GANDHI

CHAPTER TWELVE

Define the Values That Matter

From an Amish Farm to Best-Selling Author

D an Miller grew up in an Amish family where education was not valued, and opportunities outside of the local community were limited. He broke out of his childhood community and created success for himself in the larger world. Dan is the author of the New York Times best-selling *48 Days to the Work You Love* and host of the *48 Days Podcast.* As a life coach and speaker, Dan helps individuals develop a plan for integrating their dreams and passions into daily practice. Dan challenges us to ask: "What is the story you tell yourself about your experiences?" He believes the limitations of his childhood served as a springboard that compelled him to break out of the limited possibilities of his small community, although he recognizes it would have been just as easy to use those experiences as an explanation for a more limited life. If younger generation family members are going to have the opportunity to fully realize their potential as human beings and live out their dreams, that can only happen if they have absorbed the values that make their best life possible.

Our Most Important Job

I think of belief systems as something like the operating system of a computer. All the data that moves through a computer is processed through its operating system. If a computer's operating system is antiquated or defective, its functionality will be limited. If someone's belief system is defined by limiting values, they will live a limited life. If younger generation family members absorb limiting values, they will live limited lives.

Because our belief systems play such an important role in defining who we are and what we will become, shouldn't we be more conscious of what those beliefs are? While we're at it, shouldn't we consider installing new, more empowering belief systems? It is possible to be consciously proactive in defining the legacy we want to pass on, and family is the best place to do it. Family is that timeless building block of culture that must work if our civilization is to work. So, an investment of time and thought in defining and instilling positive and empowering values or belief systems in younger family members is arguably our most important task as parents, grandparents, godparents, aunts, uncles and mentors.

Our Values Limit or Liberate Us

Many American families have their own distinctive family brand that serves as a kind of collective myth that defines who they are. Psychotherapist Carl Jung once asked, "What is the myth that is managing your life?" Most of us are not fully conscious of the myths or value systems that drive us, but they are omnipresent in our lives. Like the water that surrounds a fish in the ocean, we have always been so completely immersed in these myths we may not be aware of their presence. For many of us, the myths that drive us were created organically and unintentionally over time. Those value systems were present when we emerged into the world and were infused into us by our parents and our extended family, usually without their being aware they were doing it.

Some of the beliefs we absorbed are positive and empowering, but not always. I have known families who believed they were poor and unsuccessful and always would be. Racial or cultural prejudices are also transmitted and absorbed in this way. These systems are powerful. They can be an invisible fence that keeps us trapped in a dull, limited world or they can provide a springboard that encourages us to reach for the stars.

The Stories You Tell Yourself

The values that matter most to you probably emerge from the stories you tell yourself about who you are and how you created your own success in the world. It's only natural to want to instill those values in the next generation. Sometimes, these values developed out of your own experiences; sometimes they come from the life lessons that were shared with you. They may be based on long-established religious traditions.

The examples that influenced us may also derive from negative experiences. For example, I have friends who put enormous value on not drinking alcohol because they were close to someone who was abusive when intoxicated. It is very common for my clients to tell me it is important for them to make sure their younger generation family members do not fall prey to substance abuse.

Many value systems are built around work and thriftiness. That was true in my family—hard work was an important value. At my father's funeral, a neighbor told me that my father was the hardest working person he ever knew. That's how I also remember him: he worked hard seven days a week. You had to do that on a dairy farm when you had no employees. His work ethic became a value he tried to instill in his children. The people who tell me that work ethic is an important value are the people who most frequently express concern that younger generation family members may not continue to be motivated to do productive things when they have the financial security of an inheritance.

In some families, I see values that are connected to the kind of work or business the family is in. It is not uncommon to see subtle pressure placed on younger family members to follow in the footsteps of older family members and become doctors or lawyers. In the Mississippi delta, farming is the major economic driver and that has been true for more than two hundred years. Farm families in this part of the world are celebrated at events held in their honor when that family has operated their farm for one hundred years. These are called "century farms." It's very common for farm families to encourage younger generation family members to continue the farming tradition. Quite often, they do this by creating financial incentives, such as renting the land to the family member at below market rates, to encourage these family members to pursue farming as a career choice rather than seek careers off the farm.

For me, travel is an important value. As a person who went abroad for the first time at age forty, I didn't realize how life changing an experience in a foreign culture could be. My wife and I have worked to give our children as well as other children who could not afford to travel the opportunity to discover the power of travel for themselves.

I suggest you take a few minutes and reflect on the traditions, stories, and experiences that have influenced you, positively or negatively. Those experiences are going to define the values that are important to you today. After you have done this, take a look at the list of words at the end of this chapter. Which of these resonate with you? I know many of these value words will be compelling, but make an effort to create a short list of those that resonate most powerfully with you.

As you move through this process, you may discover that one or more of these words may be associated with a particular person—someone who taught you the importance of that value, either by their positive influence or their bad behavior. I think you will find that connecting the values that matter with the people whose influence made them important will reconnect you with their stories and provide insight as to why you chose this value over others on the list. Make a note of those stories as well. They will be useful in later chapters.

Successful Families Know What is Important to Them

In the book *Beating the Midas Curse*, authors Perry Cochell and Rod Zeeb make the point that in historical surveys going all the way back to the 17th century, the families who prospered had a very clear appreciation for the values that mattered the most to them. Those values were intentionally nurtured and purposefully shared from each generation to the next. The data also showed that most adults believed values, stories, and life lessons were the most critical inheritance they could receive from their parents or leave to their children. However, only a small percentage of those responding to the surveys had taken any steps to identify those values, stories, and life lessons or to develop a strategy to intentionally pass those values on to the next generation.

What is Important to You?

In the remaining chapters I will challenge you to develop a plan to instill these important values in your younger generation family members. Before you do that, however, you have to gain some clarity around what those values are. These values will be different for every family. The next step will be to develop a plan that will help you share these values in a compelling way. There are a number of strategies that will work for you, and many of those are presented in the later chapters of this book. I have offered a wide variety of strategies because I know every family is different and every person in your family is unique. Take a look at these different approaches and choose those that will be most engaging. Involve your family in the process—it is unlikely they will take this project seriously if they are not part of developing it.

★★★★★★★★★★

I have included a link to Dan Miller's book, Forty-Eight Days to the Work you Love and a link to Dan's podcast as well. There is no shortage of literature on the importance of teaching younger generations the importance of character. I mention several of the best ones in these resource links.

www.YourAmericanLegacy.com

100 Values

IDENTIFY THE VALUES THAT ARE IMPORTANT TO YOU

From the 100 values listed below, identify the 10 that are most important to you.

Accountability	Empathy	Inquisitiveness
Accuracy	Encouragement	Integrity
Ambition	Enthusiasm	Intelligence
Balance	Environmentalism	Intuition
Care	Ethics	Justice
Cleverness	Experience	Kindness
Commitment	Faith	Knowledge
Community	Family	Leadership
Confidence	Friendship	Learning
Conservation	Frugality	Logic
Conviction	Fun	Love
Courage	Generosity	Loyalty
Creativity	Gentleness	Making a difference
Curiosity	Gratitude	Maturity
Dependability	Happiness	Modesty
Desire	Health	Motivation
Determination	Honor	Nerve
Devotion	Humility	Open-mindedness
Dignity	Humor	Optimism
Discipline	Imagination	Originality
Diversity	Independence	Patience
Duty	Individuality	Patriotism

Passion	Resourcefulness	Spontaneity
Perseverance	Respect	Stability
Popularity	Sacrifice	Success
Positivity	Satisfaction	Teaching
Power	Self-control	Temperance
Preparedness	Selflessness	Tradition
Pride	Self-reliance	Travel
Prosperity	Self-respect	Trust
Punctuality	Service	Truth
Purity	Sharing	Virtue
Reason	Shrewdness	Vision
Reliability	Sincerity	

YOUR AMERICAN LEGACY

"Your personal brand is what people say about you when you are not in the room."

– CHRIS DUCKER

CHAPTER THIRTEEN

Create Your Family Brand

What Can We Learn from McDonalds and BMW?

Branding is powerful. A brand is not just a symbol or logo. A brand is an entire package that conveys at an emotional level the kind of experience you know you will have when you purchase and consume a product. Wherever you go in the world, you know exactly what to expect if you visit a McDonalds or KFC restaurant or a Ritz Carlton hotel. A brand provides a kind of guarantee you will receive exactly what you expect. I stopped by a Starbucks in Taipei and had exactly the experience I have at the Starbucks in my own neighborhood. At BMW, you expect a very specific kind of driving experience. There is an entire engineering team in Munich that makes sure every BMW model has an exhaust system that produces that distinctive growling sound. Corporations have teams of people that focus entirely on managing their brand. Brands have value. By one estimate, the value of the Coca Cola brand is worth more than twice the annual revenues of the company.

Successful families have also developed valuable brands. In medieval times, family brands were connected to power and political influence. The Medici family first attained wealth and political power in Florence in the 13th century through its success in commerce and banking. This family dynasty lasted almost three centuries and produced three popes and a queen of France. Sometimes family brands are bound up with the products the family business produces. When we think of the Rothschild family, we think of banking. We connect the Ford family with automobiles, the Mars family with candy and the Walton family with Wal-Mart stores.

Family brands are not always connected to business. Public service is an important part of the brand in some families. I've lost count of the number of Kennedys that have held public office or served with non-profit organizations. The Bush family has a political brand nurtured over four generations. I'm sure someone who is a member of the Kennedy family or the Bush family will find it easier to raise money and obtain press coverage to start a political campaign than someone who doesn't have the benefit of their family brand. If you are a potential donor or supporter, even though you don't know much about the candidate, you make the assumption this person will share the political views and behavior consistent with the brand.

Not every family has a desirable brand. You can probably think of a family you have known that was considered unreliable or dishonest. Because of that reputation, you would be reluctant to employ or do business with a member of that family even though you did not actually know anything about the traits of that individual family member. You may well make the assumption this person will behave in a way that is consistent with their family brand. This may be an unfortunate and incorrect bias, but the power of brand—or reputation—works that way.

I want to suggest here that, just as large corporations do, you can take charge of your family brand and shape it intentionally by defining the values that matter by doing very specific things to communicate those values to younger generation family members. Being associated with a positive family brand will be hugely beneficial to them. Others will open doors for them without knowing them personally because they trust the brand. The power of your family brand will be a reflection of how effectively you have communicated the values that matter to the next generation.

Values Only Have Impact When They Are Communicated

Values must be communicated in a way that ensures they are effectively absorbed. It is only then that those values become a living influence and provide the people that matter to us with the sure sense they are an integral part of something unique and special. Knowing they are a part of something larger than themselves grounds them and provides them with the security they need to move out into the world with confidence. It empowers them to contribute their own unique value to the world.

However, when that confidence is missing, all kinds of mischief can occur. The lack of emotional security that comes when a person does not belong to a family that understands its place in the world explains, at least for me, the underlying cause of crime and gang violence that is happening now in inner cities of the U.S. and in Central America.

There are many tools available to help you communicate important values.

Create a Family Mission Statement

We've all seen mission statements—they can be found on the wall or website of most businesses. We have one for our law firm and we read it aloud every Friday morning at our team meeting. By reading it aloud, every team member reaffirms their commitment to the core values that define the way we work with each other and the clients we serve. You can create a mission statement that does the same thing for your family. Your mission statement will define the values that matter to your family unit, and by connecting with it periodically, at holidays for example, your family can reaffirm its commitment to living out those values every day.

Your mission statement should be unique to your family, and it should emerge out of the thoughtful engagement of the entire family. It doesn't have to be created in one session. It may require a family retreat where, in a resort setting and with cell phones turned off, every family member is provided a real opportunity to participate. Your mission statement is not set in concrete: it can be amended as the years pass, as insights evolve and as family members marry or pass away.

If you worked through the exercise in the last chapter, you have already done much the groundwork. However, it is also helpful to look at some well-known mission statements for guidance. Your mission statement should be clear, concise and specific to your family. You will want it to be short enough so that it can be recited in about thirty seconds. I have provided some examples in the resource links to this chapter.

Create a Family Motto

When you have clarity around who your family is and what it stands for, consider creating a family motto to use as a source of quick, consistent inspiration. You can start by looking at the organizations your family members may already be a part of. It can be your family name, or you can create a team name that embodies your family's spirit. For example, if your family is from Tallahassee, but you and your spouse met at college in Louisiana, you may want to identify yourselves as the "Tallahassee Tigers." Or you may like the simplicity of your surname. It can be anything you want it to be. If you're a non-nuclear family who came together through a second marriage, circumstance, friendship, work, or in any other way, this is a good strategy to build a unifying bond around your connection with each other.

You can draw inspiration from any source. In a 2011 University of Pennsylvania commencement speech, Academy Award-Winner Denzel Washington discussed his successes by highlighting his failures. He reminded the graduating class that there would be something they would not be good at and something they may even fail at doing. He then encouraged them to never give up, to take each failure in stride, and to "fall forward." His short motto embraces the idea of perseverance and determination, and acknowledges that our success in life is determined mostly by how we react. If we react by "falling forward," we are at least that much closer to our next step.

A good friend of mine decided his clan needed a more meaningful connection to each other. With help from a few family members, he developed a code of conduct and a family motto, all of which is now introduced to younger generation family members as they reach adulthood in a rather elaborate ceremony. None of the source material came from any links to family history— the family's code of conduct and rituals are loosely based on Christian values but the actual words, motto, and ceremony were just invented. Now, however, it's all very real to the family members who have gone through the family rite-of-passage initiation.

Design a Family Crest

For centuries, the Scots have used distinctive tartan designs to identify family by the distinctive clothing they wear. My friend Lou McAlister has his family's tartan design emblazoned on his road bike as an athletic homage to his Scottish heritage. My friend Chris David became very animated telling me how his family developed their own unique family crest. Tracing their roots back to Lebanon and a journey on a ship that eventually ended in the U.S., a family team effort produced a drawing that incorporated the pivotal elements of the journey and struggle. That design then got handed off to an artist who produced a professional version. The design is now displayed on a family flag that flies in Chris' back lawn. The photo of the David family flag is in the resource link to this chapter.

Designs like the one Chris' family developed can also be turned into lapel pins and other artistic expressions that can be worn or displayed. When these designs are the product of authentic family engagement, they can provide a real connection to the history and values that come with belonging to your tribe. I have provided some links to companies that will take your family's artistic efforts and transform them into professional quality jewelry that will someday become a family heirloom.

Create an Ethical Will

While there are many things you can do with your family now, there are other things that you can do that can be shared after you are gone. A good example is an ethical will. The word "will" can be confusing because it is used to refer to several different kinds of documents that accomplish different purposes. The most common meaning of the term "will" is a legal document that passes property and other financial assets to heirs upon death.

A living will is quite different from a traditional will. It defines a person's desires about end of life decisions such as withdrawing life support if the maker of the living will has a terminal medical condition and is not consciously able to communicate those end of life desires. Living wills are a fairly recent planning tool but they have quickly become a routine component of most estate plans.

Ethical wills, while not used as commonly today as legal wills or living wills, nonetheless have a three-thousand-year history. Stated succinctly, while legal wills deal with the valuables, ethical wills deal with the values. Ethical wills should be used more frequently. An ethical will is a document created by a senior generation family member to provide instruction to younger family members and future generations on how to lead a moral life. Ethical wills do not have a specific format, but they generally give the author the opportunity to reflect on themes from their past with personal stories and lessons. They also reflect on current personal values and beliefs, expressions of faith, love, and gratitude, and sometimes apologies. They also provide advice, blessings, hopes, and dreams for future generations.

Creating an ethical will is a positive exercise that gives you the opportunity to learn about yourself, reflect on your life, and affirm what others mean to you. It can contain historical information, stories, family histories and truths that are difficult to express. It can open the door to forgiveness and allow you to come to terms with your own mortality. Creating an ethical will can be a spiritual experience for the author and can also provide a sense of completion and closure that makes your departure easier for your family when the time comes.

I know that for most of us, starting at a blank computer screen to create an ethical will is challenging. I have provided some resources in the links at the end of this chapter that can make that task much easier.

Write Legacy Letters

A legacy letter is similar in concept to an ethical will. However, it is usually written to one person. In this letter, you take the opportunity to share specific insights, wisdom, and advice with that person. You can create several legacy letters, each directed to a specific person, which contain your wisdom and insight based on your knowledge of that person's strengths and weakness. I have provided some examples of legacy letters in the resource links at the end of this chapter.

Write Your Trustee a Letter of Wishes

I am an advocate of trustee letter of wishes, and I will explain why. Most estate plans I create for clients provide that assets are left to heirs in discretionary trusts to protect them from divorce, creditors and sometimes, the financial or emotional immaturity of the heir. In many cases, the trustee of that trust is someone other than the beneficiary of the trust or a family member that knows the beneficiary well.

Naming an outside trustee, usually a bank or trust company, is done when our client makes the determination that someone unrelated to the family who has the professional skill set to manage assets and make distribution decisions is more well suited than a family member to serve in that role. In my practice, about one-third of the trustees named to serve in that role are non-family members. When that is the case, I believe the trustee needs to be provided some insight that explains why the creator of the trust chose an outside trustee for this role. Quite often, it is a concern about the beneficiary's spending habits, addictions or the stability of the beneficiary's marriage. This is understandably sensitive information, but after the creator of the trust is gone, the trustee is at a decided disadvantage if they do not have this information available to guide decisions, particularly decisions about distributions from the trust.

It is common knowledge in the professional trustee community that beneficiaries with drug, alcohol or gambling addictions often show up in the trustee's office looking very presentable and make a passionate and convincing case for distributions. A thoughtful trustee letter can provide insight about the beneficiary the trustee can refer to for guidance as they consider whether or not to honor that request.

You know your beneficiaries better than anyone. You can draft a letter to the trustee that provides specific insight on that beneficiary's strengths and weaknesses. You may point out, for example, that the trustee be attentive to drug, alcohol or marital issues. By coordinating the language in your trustee letter with flexible distribution language in your trust document, your trustee can be given the flexibility to condition distributions from the trust to specific performance objectives, such as graduation from college or earning a minimum level of income from work. The insight you provide in your trustee letter will allow the trustee to evaluate distribution requests through the lens of your deep knowledge about that beneficiary long after you are gone. Your trustee letter can be kept in the trustee's files and reviewed anytime your beneficiary makes a request for a distribution. We provide examples of trustee letters to our clients and encourage them to create their own version based on their insights about their beneficiaries. I have provided some examples of trustee letters in the resource link to this chapter.

Family Engagement in the Process is the Key to Success

As you can see, there are a variety of ways to communicate the values that matter to you. You should also know that the more engagement you have with family members in the process, the more effective your strategy will be. If you present your strategy without any input from family members in final form on stone tablets, it will not be as fully embraced as it would be if the strategy is developed around the dining table or at a resort where everyone can engage creatively in the project with you.

If you make the effort to work through this collaboratively, you will discover younger generation family members will be excited to engage in this process with you. The result will be a deeper bond between family members and an enhanced commitment to live out the most enduring values. Your family brand can be respected and endure long after you are gone.

★★★★★★★★★★

The resource links to this chapter are extensive. There are links to companies that will help you produce a professional quality family crest, create an ethical will, write legacy letters and a trustee letter of wishes and much more. I have also included a photograph of my friend Chris David's family crest.

www.YourAmericanLegacy.com

AMERICAN LEGACY

"Stories have to be told or they die, and when they die, we can't remember who we are or why we're here."

— SUE MONK KIDD, AUTHOR OF THE SECRET LIFE OF BEES

CHAPTER FOURTEEN

Preserve Family History, Stories & Legends

An Evening at the Amphitheater

The sun had just set on a cool Mediterranean night. The sky was clear and dark, and stars were beginning to emerge in the new night sky; the glimmer of fire in the large ceramic pots bathed the amphitheater gates with an air of mystery that stoked anticipation. The overflowing crowd gathered inside. The gentle sound of waves against the shore reminded those waiting that the mystery and might of the sea lay just beyond the scent of the cedar trees. The evening breeze over the water had already chased away the balmy day air as a crescent moon rose into the night sky on the low horizon.

Tonight was special. The featured storyteller was a legend: his recitations were passionate and compelling. He could deliver the entire evening's performance from memory. Most people in the audience had heard these stories since childhood, but they were more than willing to pay the substantial admission to listen to these epic Homeric legends recited again. The hero stepped down from the stars to relive his adventures. His mythic journey to exotic foreign places still resonated with the audience because his encounters with sea monsters was also part of their story, only more colorful. The legends he spoke of were a reminder that, in the end, the journey would be successful, and worth the effort and the risk.

Storytelling is Ancient and Universal

Storytelling is an ancient art, and not just in Greece. For most of human history, people did not have literacy skills, so stories were the primary vehicle used by older generations to pass values, culture, and life lessons to the younger generations. The epic poem *The Lusiads*, written and recited in Homeric fashion, celebrates the exploits of Vasco da Gama, the Portuguese hero responsible for establishing the sea route to India. Native Americans shared their creation stories and tales of legendary ancestors around fires with younger members of their tribes. In Iceland, epic dramatic sagas written a thousand years ago and recited today in the ancient Icelandic language preserve the solidarity and identity of a unique culture carved out of ice and struggle.

Jesus of Nazareth made quite an impact on the world, and as far as we know, he never wrote a book or even a blog post. His message was initially shared in stories and parables communicated in sermons. After his death, these stories were spread around the known world by disciples who were almost certainly not literate. The early Christian church was launched with the oral telling and retelling of the story of Jesus' life, death, and resurrection—the written version came much later. Much of the power of the written version—the New Testament—is in stories that were originally shared orally.

Storytelling has been effective throughout human history. Our most celebrated heroes were great storytellers. Abraham Lincoln could mesmerize audiences with an endless repertoire of folk tales from the backwoods of Kentucky and Illinois. Ronald Reagan's speeches were memorable in large part because of the poignant stories of average Americans woven into them.

Any native Texan boy or girl can tell you of Texas' independent and adventurous history. Some people believe that when young Texans are immersed at a young age in the stories of state legends fighting and dying against impossible odds, seeds are planted that encourage a greater willingness to take large risks when they reach adulthood. That risk-taking mindset is reflected today in the corporate boardrooms of Dallas, Houston, and Austin. In Texas, success is celebrated, not resented, and failure is viewed as temporary. There is no shortage of stories of a bankrupt oilman who rises up, dusts himself off, and goes on to become a legend. All this history comes together at the Alamo in downtown San Antonio, which is quite purposefully managed like a religious shrine. Nurtured by these larger than life legends, it is not surprising that young Texans grow into adults with an outsized sense of personal confidence and potential.

Stories are powerful. This Aboriginal proverb makes the point that great preachers and politicians have learned and practiced:

Tell me a fact and I'll learn.

Tell me a truth and I'll believe.

Tell me a story and it will live in my heart forever.

Storytelling Technology is Better Now

The tools and technology of storytelling have become more powerful. In the 1930s and 1940s, families would gather around the one radio in their home and listen to tales of *Little Orphan Annie and Captain Midnight*. Today, I watch movies on my laptop or my iPhone on long flights.

The English-speaking world gained a contemporary epic with J.R.R. Tolkien's trilogy *The Lord of the Rings*. He created entire cultures—characters, maps, and languages—to highlight the value of the individual. The movie trilogy was successful because the everyman—the little guy—was the hero. In one scene, the viewer sees young hobbit Frodo Baggins standing beside the square-jawed hero as they face the daunting challenge of returning the ring of power that had been lost for over two thousand years to the volcano at Mordor where it must be destroyed so humanity could be saved. Who would accept the responsibility and carry the ring to its destiny? Popular culture would assume the natural choice would be the tall, good-looking hero, but Tolkien does not see it that way. It is the ordinary man, Frodo, who steps up and becomes the hero of the story. "I will bear the ring," he says, and he does.

Frodo's journey is fraught with countless dangers, including orcs, wraiths, and volcanoes. However, his true test will be much more than the perilous journey to Mordor—he must also conquer his inner struggles by not giving in to the ring's temptations of power. Frodo, pure in heart though he was, was not invulnerable to those temptations. His desire to hold on to the ring almost consumed him, until, in a final fight, Gollum tears the ring from Frodo. In the melee, the ring is cast into the volcano. The imperfect Frodo returns back to the shire, only to find he is too traumatized to remain there. Frodo's strengths and weaknesses teach a dual lesson—the individual can accomplish great feats, but every choice has a price. Sometimes doing what is right requires a sacrifice.

Your Family's Stories are the Most Powerful Stories

Stories and legends have the power to influence our lives. However, those stories that have the most power are your stories and those of your ancestors. I am influenced daily by the stories I learned as a child about my family. Neither of my parents graduated from high school. My father quit school at age twelve to help support his family. An Independence Day firecracker damaged my mother's eyesight during the Summer after the tenth grade, and the family couldn't afford glasses for her, so she dropped out of school.

My parents were dairy farmers who worked rented land while dreaming of owning their own farm. In 1948, a farm they wanted became available, but they didn't have the money to buy it. As luck would have it, an in-law offered to loan them the small sum they needed to make the purchase. My parents abhorred even the thought of debt, but knew there was no other way to buy that farm. So, they borrowed the money.

In the late 1940s, cattle feed was still distributed in hundred pound sacks, not in bulk trucks as it is today. The sacks were made from a kind of crude linen material, and the manufacturer would apply their brand to the sacks with generous quantities of brightly colored paint that was impossible to remove.

My parents decided not to purchase anything beyond the essentials—food and coffee—until they had paid off the loan, so my mother began making dresses from these colorfully painted feed sacks. They made for interesting couture in rural Arkansas; they were durable and no doubt a topic of conversation.

Within eighteen months of buying the farm, my parents called the relative that had generously loaned them the money and asked if they could meet him at the bank. In that short time, they had saved enough money to pay the mortgage in full. This story has been told often in my family. It became code for "stop complaining and get to work." It also conveyed the message: "Don't borrow money unless you have no other choice."

Why People Succeed

In one of the most watched Ted Talks of all time, University of Pennsylvania professor Angela Duckworth explores the question of why some people succeed, while others don't. After listing all the reasons we typically identify as the factors that influence success—education, intelligence, physical attractiveness and family connections—she reveals the results of her research. It turns out the most reliable predictor of success was something that can be best defined as "grit." I'm sure she is right about this. My parents lacked education and money, but they both had an oversupply of grit and were successful in all the ways I define it.

Simple Stories Can Be Powerful

Our stories don't have to be grand or heroic. In fact, those that are most effective in conveying useful life lessons are often simple stories about very ordinary things. The messages these stories convey can make a huge difference in the lives of younger generation family members.

Washing My Grandmother's Mercedes

My friend Dustin Kenyon shared the story of his relationship with his grandfather with me. His grandparents would make the drive from California to Salt Lake to visit a few times each year when Dustin was a child. Over time, it became a ritual that he and his grandfather would clean and wash his grandmother's Mercedes before the return trip, and it was always an activity Dustin's grandfather reserved just for him. He describes how he and his grandfather took great care to clean and vacuum the inside of the car as well as wash and polish the outside, always paying very careful attention to every detail. Dustin became misty-eyed when he shared with me that he finally realized this activity was not about taking care of his grandmother's car—it was Dustin's grandfather's way of teaching him how to love and care for the wife he would eventually have.

Stories provide instruction and remind us that these people who are now frail and aging, or deceased, were once young, scared, scrappy, and mischievous. The stories imparted to us tell us about misadventures with alcohol, economic or psychological depression, war, struggle, faith, failure, and success. We need these stories to teach us who we are and instill the confidence we need to assure us of our rightful place in the order of things. Through these stories, we learn who we want to be.

Selling Eggs on the Telephone

This short anecdote was shared with me when I was a teenager by my uncle and the story made an outsized impact on me, although I doubt my uncle remembers the conversation. He was in the hatching egg business. That industry is more technology-driven that you might think, and even a few decades ago, significant genetic science was involved in producing eggs that would eventually become the chickens that would become Kentucky Fried Chicken. The goal was to hatch an egg that produced a chicken that could reach a particular target weight quicker than a competing strain sold by a competitor. Reaching target weight faster was huge, as feeding millions of these birds an extra two or three days was costly.

The problem; however, was that all eggs looked the same. There was no way to tell if an egg was from one of the new, more advanced genetic strains or from an older, slower-growing strain. My uncle was in charge of selling these eggs to customers around the country.

One day, he told me something that struck me. He told me that the thing he was most proud of in his career was that he could pick up the phone and sell eggs to anyone because they believed him when he told them what they were buying. They wouldn't know for months if they got the genetic strain they purchased, but they trusted he was telling them the truth. I have no doubt he always did. For me, that was the definition of integrity. It made me want to be the kind of guy that commands that level of trust.

Knowing Your Family History May Make Your Children More Successful

A group of psychologists from Emory University developed a test called the "Do You Know" test. It's a simple twenty-question test that was given to children to learn how much they knew about their parents and grandparents and was part of a larger research project studying the emotional resiliency of children. It turns out that of all the factors they studied, the child's score on the "Do You Know" test was the single best predictor of emotional resiliency.

Author Bruce Feiler makes the point that we should not airbrush family history and be reluctant to share the negative or unflattering family stories with younger generation family members. He suggests the stories we tell should "oscillate." By that, he means the positive or heroic stories should be counter-balanced with stories of failure and disappointment. Our children learn from our failures just as they learn from our successes.

What Happens When You Don't Have a Story?

Not everyone has a story, or if they have it, they may not know it. The 2016 movie *Lion* tells the true story of a five-year-old Indian boy who goes to sleep in a parked train car and wakes up to find the train moving. The train travels more than eight hundred miles before it stops in a strange city on the other side of India where a different language is spoken. The boy has no way to contact his mother and he couldn't recall the name of the town where he lived. He is eventually adopted by a very decent Australian family and grows into young adulthood. By chance, while at a party with his girlfriend, he connects with the aroma of a food that reminds him of something his mother had prepared for him as a child. That neural connection triggered a compelling, multi-year obsession to reconnect with his Indian family. It's a poignant film, and it reminds us just how powerful the urge is to know and connect with our own life's story.

For decades, state legislatures have passed laws preventing adopted persons from learning about their biological families. Not only have adoptees been cut off from potentially valuable medical information, they have been denied access to an important piece of their personal story. We are now seeing a movement around the country to provide greater access to this information.

When lack of personal stories creates a vacuum in our lives, we find ways to fill it. Often, the things we fill it with are less than productive. When I read accounts of shootings that happen daily in the ghettos of Los

Angeles, Chicago, and Little Rock, I'm inclined to think the young people committing those crimes are probably not people who have internalized the heroic stories of their proud ancestors. I believe one way we can change the destiny of these communities is by finding ways to connect these young people with these empowering stories. Even if we can't find those stories, we can help them create a more compelling personal narrative rather than living out the images of scarcity and impoverishment that drive their behavior now.

Preserving Your Stories is Easier than Ever

Your story matters. It matters to you more than you may realize, and knowing your story is critical for the young people in your family who are working to define their place in the world. You may be around to tell those stories when they are ready, but it is possible that you will not be here to participate in that important task. I encourage you to start organizing your stories and capture them permanently, so they are available to younger generations of family members at that moment when they are ready to hear them. That may not happen until they are in their twenties or when they have their first child, but there will be a time when they will need to hear your stories. In the last few years, there has been an explosion of technology solutions that make capturing and preserving stories easy and inexpensive. I suggest a few solutions in this chapter, but I also provide an extensive list of resources in the link at the end of this chapter.

Video and Audio Recordings

I encourage every client that works with us to allow us to record a video or audio interview with them. A couple weeks before the interview, I provide them with a "conversation guide" to set the framework for the discussion. These conversations are insightful and sometimes emotional. While our interviews are generally unedited, there are professional video companies that can create a more professional, edited version. Some of these have a History Channel look and feel, complete with music and relevant historical film footage incorporated into the final product.

iPhone and Android Apps

There are many apps that work on iPhones and Androids that make it easy to create recordings on the spot. These apps provide suggested questions and frameworks for the interview. Some of these are free and others can be purchased inexpensively. I provide a list of several of these apps in the resource links to this chapter.

Scrapbooks

The old-fashioned art of scrapbooking can be quite effective in telling the family story when the books are organized and assembled thoughtfully. It's important for the contents to be properly curated so the photographs, newspaper clippings, and other elements are preserved with materials that will last over time. You can create these scrapbooks yourself or bring in someone with experience to help you. I suggest some resources for scrapbooking in the resource links to this chapter.

Vacation books

My wife and I started creating vacation books a decade ago when the technology was still cumbersome. As time has passed, the options have expanded and the books have become less expensive. We appreciate the books more as time passes. They reconnect us with great experiences in faraway places and provide us with a way to share those experiences with others. There are several good sources for creating these books. I have listed some we like in the resource links to this chapter.

Use a Family Historian to Document Your Family Story

In most communities in the U.S., you can find individuals that can help you research your family history and develop a written narrative of your family's story. If you find researching family history and composing the story into a written format to be intimidating, a family historian can be a useful and inexpensive resource. I provide information to help you locate a family historian in the resource link below.

If you are more ambitious, you can document your family's history in a coffee table quality book that is printed on high quality paper and bound professionally. I have reviewed some of these books, and they are impressive but not inexpensive to produce. I have also provided some links to individuals who can help you produce books of this quality.

Write Your Own Book

Richard was one of my most interesting clients. He would sometimes come by my office for no reason and share war stories about aerial combat in the South Pacific during World War II. He also shared stories about his later career in civilian aviation. One day, he came by and asked if he could give me something. As I brought him into my office, he reached into his bag and pulled out a book and handed it to me. "Here's the book I wrote," he said. "This is something I've wanted to do for a while, so I decided to just do it."

"You wrote a book?" I asked.

"Well, I didn't actually write it. I talked it. The writer spent a few days at my kitchen table while I told him all the stories I've been telling you, and he put them together to make this book. If somebody had told me to sit down at a computer and write a book, it would never have happened. But I just sat at my kitchen table and told stories. Some of them were embarrassing—I put some takeaways in there too, like lessons I learned the hard way. I thought, if my grandkids read this, maybe they'll avoid making some of the same mistakes I made."

Richard's book will never make the *New York Times* Best Seller list, but I'm sure Richard's great grandchildren will be reading this book a century from now, and that is the audience that matters most to him. My publisher tells me that books like this are becoming much more common. The author's job is to organize the stories and recollections that had an impact on the life of the storyteller and then draw out the life lessons that are important enough to share. The writer then put the words on the page. This process makes actually writing a book a realistic and enjoyable project. This is one of the most powerful ways you can preserve your story. I have provided a link in the resource materials that will give additional insight into the process of writing your own book.

Your Story is Their Story

Choose an approach to capturing your story that works for you. I think you will discover what I discovered—family members of all ages become surprisingly engaged in this activity. Your story is also their story, and they understand that.

★★★★★★★★★★

My team and I have curated an extensive list of resources that provide a myriad of ways you can preserve your family's story. We have links to books, Ted Talks, telephone apps, resources for creating you own family scrapbook or travel book. And there is much more.

www.YourAmericanLegacy.com/resources

YOUR AMERICAN LEGACY

"Our most treasured family heirlooms are our sweet family memories. The past is never dead, it is not even past."

—WILLIAM FAULKNER

CHAPTER FIFTEEN

Your Heirloom Assets Are Powerful: Use Them Creatively

From Pompeii to the Peloponnesus

P ompeii was a flourishing resort frequented by ancient Rome's most affluent citizens. Elaborate villas lined the paved streets. The small factories, artisans' shops, taverns, cafes, brothels, and bathhouses were thriving on the eve of the eruption of Mt. Vesuvius in 79 AD. Superheated poison gas and pulverized rock barreled down the side of the mountain and consumed everything and everyone in its path. By the time the eruption ended the next day, Pompeii was buried under millions of tons of volcanic ash until it was discovered in 1748 by a group of explorers looking for ancient artifacts. It was exactly as it had been 1700 years before. Human skeletons were right where they'd fallen, forever frozen in an instant, tragic sculpture. Everyday objects and household goods littered the streets. The buildings were also intact. Pompeii played an important role in the neo-Classical revival of the eighteenth century when Europe's wealthiest and most fashionable families displayed art objects or reproductions of those art objects from the ruins. The drawings of Pompeii's buildings helped shape the architectural trends of the era. Today, Pompeii is a World Heritage Site, and fascination with its ruins is as great as ever. These ruins, and the artifacts taken from them, provide an up close and personal window into the sometimes uncomfortably intimate lives of these ancient ancestors.

My partner Tom Ray spends his summers as a team leader on an archeological dig in the Greek Peloponnese peninsula. This location was a thriving city thirty-five hundred years ago. Tom became very animated in telling me about this experience. He showed me his pictures of the site as he explained how the very exacting excavation process works. During one conversation with him, I asked him why they go to all this trouble just to dig up old kitchen utensils. He was a bit irritated by my question. "Archaeology is more than just the artifacts," he said. "The artifacts taken together paint a picture that helps modern people see how *similar* we are to past societies, not just our differences. We learn about our present through studying our past, and it helps us understand how our present can profoundly affect future generations."

Artifacts Don't Have to Be Ancient to Make an Impact

Even as recently as our great-grandparents' time, the way people traveled, plowed their fields, cooked their meals, and entertained themselves is almost unrecognizable to us today. The artifacts from that time—found in museums like the Smithsonian in Washington D.C., Greenfield Village in Detroit, and in hundreds of smaller museums all around America—reveal a life that was radically different than our own, and those artifacts are only a few generations removed from us.

Washington, D.C.'s Holocaust Memorial Museum uses artifacts and remembrances of survivors to tell the story of the systematic liquidation of more than six million Jews by Nazi Germany and its collaborators. The guiding force behind the founding of this museum was the late Elie Wiesel, who was motivated by the fear that if the Holocaust story and artifacts were not preserved and shared with younger generations, the experience would be forgotten and then be repeated.

The Most Powerful Artifacts Are Your Artifacts

While museum artifacts interest us, the most engaging artifacts are the ones that are handed down to us by our own ancestors. For our children and grandchildren, these may be the everyday things we are using now, and we probably do not see them as artifacts at all. However, these tangible things take on significance when they are connected to stories of challenge and struggle. Maybe they just offer a window into your life, but your grandchildren will want to know about your life, no matter how ordinary it may seem to you. What do you have that would be useful in telling your story? It may be jewelry, old weapons, military uniforms or furniture. I once mediated the division of a family's collection of handmade quilts. Quilting is popular in my part of the country, and many of these quilts are designed to preserve a family story or celebrate a family tradition. Artifacts like these need to be preserved because they can serve as a voice that shares our stories when we are no longer here to share them ourselves.

The Grandmother's Engagement Ring

A colleague of mine took his children to visit his elderly mother in the Midwest. The trip coincided with his oldest daughter's sixteenth birthday. While there, the grandmother took her granddaughter to her bedroom and told her the story of how she met her husband—the girl's grandfather— who had already passed. She told her about the Great Depression and how, when they met, her grandfather had only an old Model "A" Ford and just enough money to afford an engagement ring with a diamond barely large enough to see.

She slowly removed the ring from her finger and explained that the ring represented the beginning of everything that came after—a successful marriage, a business, and family. She then paused and moved a bit closer. She reached out to her granddaughter and said, "It's your sixteenth birthday. Today I'm giving you this ring. But it won't be yours forever. When the next girl in our family has her sixteenth birthday, it will be your responsibility to give her this ring and tell her this story."

What Every Estate Planning Attorney Knows

The death of a family member is a stressful time. The process of arranging for the funeral, writing the obituary, and then settling the affairs of the deceased can be challenging because family members have to work together to make decisions that are outside the scope of their everyday lives. Quite often, the grief from the recent loss and the stress of the moment provides a venue where ancient childhood grievances and jealousies can resurface and complicate otherwise straightforward decisions.

Ask any estate planning attorney what causes most of the family arguments, and you won't have to wait long for an answer: it's the division of tangible property when someone dies. Arguments can break out over the division of property that has little or no economic value. It's not about the dollar value of the item—it's the emotional connection to the item that matters. I encourage clients to identify all the items of tangible property that could possibly be a source of conflict, make a handwritten list describing the item, and name the individual who they want designated to receive it. Most states now allow that a handwritten list can be legally incorporated by reference into a last will and testament or a revocable living trust. Generally, the memorandum can be completed at home without witnesses and without a notary. It doesn't work for money, securities, or intangibles, but it definitely works for the heirloom objects that cause most of the arguments.

In my practice, I use document creation technology created by WealthCounsel, the company I mentioned in Chapter Two, to produce a form for the handwritten memorandums our clients use to designate the names of the recipients of these tangible items. There are over five thousand attorneys in the U.S. using this document creation technology platform, and virtually all of them provide this kind of memorandum to their clients. In my practice, we review our clients' estate plans every year, and I have made this tangible personal property memorandum part of our annual review process. Providing a clear set of instructions on who is to receive these heirloom items is a critical component in preserving family harmony. I recall specifically how two relatives of mine became estranged because one of them removed some glass fruit jars from my grandfather's home when he passed. Those items, I'm guessing, had a value of less than five dollars, but it took ten years for the relationship to heal.

While I think a memorandum designating the recipients of these items is a good idea and one that is very easy to execute, it's not the best idea. The better solution, I believe, is to identify specific items of tangible personal property and develop a separate letter (handwritten or typed and signed) that tells the story of that item with an explanation of why you chose that person to receive it. The letter can contain a story or life lesson that is appropriate for that person. I like to point out to my clients that doing this costs nothing because they already own the heirloom asset. It does require an investment of some effort and imagination.

Technology is Changing How We Preserve the Past

The late President George H.W. Bush produced a memoir in 2014 that received very good reviews. The book contained letters between himself and his wife Barbara dating back to 1941. Apparently, the Bushes had kept this correspondence in filing cabinets where it was available as a resource as he wrote his memoir. I mention this because a number of commentators have suggested that memoirs like this will likely not be written in the future because our correspondence is done using emails and text messages which we usually do not save.

With phones now equipped with cameras, people are taking more photos than ever. But will those photos be around in fifty, or even twenty, years? We know video footage taken twenty years ago will soon disintegrate unless it is permanently preserved. Years from now, when we look back on our lives and reflect on the things that matter, will we have the photos and artifacts to reconnect us to the memories? Those things can now be lost forever, because someone hit the delete button or reformatted a hard-drive. However, they don't have to disappear. The marketplace is responding to the need to preserve our own historic resources, including digital files. I have provided a list of helpful resources in the link below.

★★★★★★★★★★

Personal artifacts are much more important than most people realize. I have provided some examples of useful ways to use tangible personal property as a value transmitter. And just to underscore my point, I have included links to several museums around the United States where you can see how artifacts are used to tell America's story...which is also your story.

www.YourAmericanLegacy.com/resources

YOUR AMERICAN LEGACY

"We not only nurture our sacred relationships through ritual, but we are nurtured by them as well. In ritual, we move, and we are moved."

—ALISON LEIGH LILLY

CHAPTER SIXTEEN

Make the Most of Family Rituals and Ceremonies

What Can Five Thousand Years of Jewish Tradition Teach Us?

I remember seeing *The Ten Commandments* in the theatre when I was a small boy. It made quite an impression on me. What an incredible idea! The image of God parting the Red Sea on the command of Charlton Heston was seared into my head. This movie predated the development of computer generated graphics by decades, but the visual image of the waters separating, creating a dry path for God's people to escape Pharaoh's army was still impressive. And the underlying idea—that God would dramatically intervene to protect his chosen people, allowing them to escape generations of bondage, was so compelling it has continued to be celebrated every year in Jewish homes and synagogues all around the world.

I am not Jewish, but I know enough about the history and culture of Judaism to know that it dates back more than five thousand years. I also know that, at various times in history, Jews have been a people under siege. The history of Jewish culture includes dramatic stories of persecution. Over six million Jews were sent to the gas chambers in Nazi Germany before and during World War II. In the fall of 2018, we recall the tragic shooting at the Tree of Life Synagogue in Pittsburgh where eleven members of the synagogue were killed.

Thriving Jewish communities exist in most cities in the world. What fascinates me is how Jewish culture has survived and thrived over the centuries despite the global dispersion and the often-threatening local political environments. I believe the rituals that are so deeply embedded in Jewish religious ceremonies and family life provide us with the explanation of this persistent survival. Religious Jews observe a weekly tradition called Shabbat. Shabbat observance begins a few minutes before sunset on Friday and continues until three stars appear in the sky on Saturday night. Shabbat begins with the lighting of candles and reciting a blessing on Friday evenings. The tradition includes blessings, meals served at specific times, and time spent with the family. Family members are expected to be present for Shabbat.

Jews celebrate a number of religious holidays throughout the year, but one of the most widely celebrated is Passover, which commemorates the biblical story of Exodus that is celebrated in *The Ten Commandments*. Jews see Passover as a celebration of freedom. Every year, they retell the Passover story during Passover Seder, which is a feast held during the holiday. The Seder is always observed on the first night of Passover, and in some homes on the second night as well.

During Seder, participants take part in a ceremonial dinner that includes symbolic foods accompanied by the retelling of the Passover story. This experience is multi-sensory: it includes the smell, taste, and touch of the food, the physical participation in the ceremony, the sound of Hebrew being spoken, and the emotional power of the epic story of God liberating his people from bondage. It's easy to see how younger members of the congregation absorb this experience.

The Catholic Mass: A Multi-Sensory Experience

The Roman Catholic Church dates back to the earliest days of organized Christianity. It currently has over one billion members, and by any standard one of the most successful organizations of all time. The history of the Roman Catholic Church is not without its dark periods, but in spite of that, this organization has endured and grown to become the largest institution on earth. How do we explain this success and persistent durability over time?

There are many explanations, of course, but I want to offer a simple one: the power of the Catholic mass. Mass is offered daily to many Catholics but, more commonly, mass is attended weekly on Saturday evening or Sunday. The mass includes elements of the sacraments that, when experienced as part of the worship experience, touch participants in every way a human can be accessed—sight, sound, smell, taste, and touch. With daily or weekly encounters with these elements, the accompanying message is infused into parishioners and absorbed at a level that goes far deeper than mere intellectual understanding. I know people who are no longer active Catholics who question many of the church's practices. However, most of them concede that being brought up in a Catholic family—being a "cradle Catholic"—means they can never fully leave the church because it is so much a part of who they are. We know also that many who leave the church eventually return later in life because of the enduring connection made during childhood.

Call Signs and Other Examples

Rituals from religious traditions create a powerful bond that preserves the connection between the individual and the institution. But religions don't have a monopoly on the use of rituals. There are many other examples. College fraternities and sororities build a lifelong bond with members through their initiation rites. Masonic Lodges have effectively used secret rituals that date back centuries. Successful corporations have recognized the power of ritual and ceremony to create a bond with employees and advance the mission of the business.

My son received his call sign from his Navy flight squadron after months of very serious deliberation by the entire squadron who considered over thirty possible names. My son had no choice in the matter. The squadron chose his call sign as he waited outside the room while his squadron deliberated. After the decision was made, he was then called into the room to have it revealed to him. I later noticed the members of his squadron and other squadrons almost always refer to each other by their call sign and not their given names. I was struck by this. Squadrons actually give their members new identities that last a lifetime. That name permanently connects the member to the squadron and to the larger social ecosystem of the U.S. Navy.

The Power of Ritual & Ceremony

Every successful culture has incorporated the use of ritual and ceremony. Weddings are not merely a legal arrangement: they are occasions of celebration where words are spoken and promises are made in the presence of family and community. Politicians and Supreme Court justices do not just sign some paperwork in order to take office. They are sworn in, usually in front of a crowd of citizens who hear their public commitment to faithfully uphold the duties of the office.

We humans need these rituals. In the absence of a healthy ritual system—in religion, military or public life, or in families—cults and gangs find a foothold with the untethered members of society who crave a sense of belonging to something larger than themselves.

What I am suggesting here is that we identify and elevate the significance of healthy rituals. If these rituals do not exist, we can create them. We know the most powerful rituals connect with all five senses. We have real evidence rituals and ceremonies work to preserve institutions. They can also preserve an enduring connection between family members.

Our Christmas Ritual

At Christmas, every member of my family receives a brown paper bag filled with candy, fruit, and nuts. The bag has the recipient's name written on it with a marker. We give each other gifts too, but everyone gets their own brown paper bag. When I was a young boy, my mother thought it was dishonest to tell us our gifts came from Santa Claus, so our presents were placed under the tree several days early where they teased and tempted my younger brother and me. One year, curiosity got the best of us, and after several annoying requests, my mother relented and told us we could open our gifts right then—two days before Christmas. When Christmas morning came, my brother and I were a bit downtrodden knowing there was nothing left under the tree to open. But we were wrong—my father had decided that something should be under the tree for us on Christmas morning, and that's when we discovered the brown paper bag with our names written on it. Every Christmas after that, everyone in our family got a brown bag with their name on it. When we got married, our spouses got a bag. When we had children, each child got a bag. That bag came to represent the idea that you belong. If you got a brown paper bag with your name on it, you knew you were an essential part of the family.

Rites of Passage

Most cultures provide rite of passage rituals as a way of ceremonializing the transition from adolescence to adulthood or providing valuable psychological preparation for important life transitions. The concept of a vision quest appears in many cultures, including days spent alone in a wilderness where the person has the opportunity to contemplate the significance of his or her life and the meaning of adulthood or the life mission ahead. Sometimes these quests require completing strenuous physical or mental challenges. The Christian New Testament describes how Jesus spent forty days and forty nights in the Judean wilderness spiritually preparing himself for his ministry. These rites are expressed in religious ceremonies such as Confirmation in many Christian traditions, a Bar or Bat Mitzvah in Jewish culture, and circumcision in both Jewish and Islamic cultures.

In recognizing that these rituals meet an important psychological need, some commentators have suggested that Protestant Christianity has missed opportunities by diminishing the significance of these rites of passage. Several modern protestant pastors have initiated new programs in their congregations to fill this gap. In his book, *Raising a Modern-Day Knight*, author and pastor Robert Lewis developed a program for young men that includes rituals, ceremonies, and time spent on vision quest type experiences with adult men in the congregation who serve as mentors. Authors Doreen Hanna and Pam Farrel have created a similar model for young women which is outlined in their book, *Raising a Modern-Day Princess*.

Create or Elevate Traditions in Your Family

In a culture that celebrates casualness, the power of rituals and traditions has been in decline. I suggest that it would be beneficial to reverse this trend, and intentionally install rituals and traditions in family life or to find existing traditions and purposefully enhance or deepen them. There is no shortage of material from which to create or expand family traditions.

Many families have them and don't recognize them—it's just the way they do things. There are traditions around holidays, the celebration of birthdays, and celebrations of ethnic ancestry. They almost always include some kind of food or drink that is associated with that occasion. Some of these have religious or cultural roots. Some have just emerged. They all have the potential to be enhanced and celebrated more purposefully. These rituals can become a powerful connector of family members to each other and to the deeper values the family represents.

★★★★★★★★★★

Just as the practice of rituals has allowed religious institutions and cultures to survive and thrive for millennia, the intentional practice of rituals in your family can do the same. You don't have to figure this out by yourself. The resource links to this chapter provide a very helpful roadmap. There are Ted Talks and books from various traditions. Because food is such an important part of family ritual, I have included a link to Katie Jacobs book, "So Much to Celebrate: Entertaining the ones you Love".

www.YourAmericanLegacy.com/resources

YOUR AMERICAN LEGACY

*"The world is a book, and those who do
not travel read only a page."*

—Saint Augustine

CHAPTER SEVENTEEN

Discover the Power of Travel

From Hot Springs to Hanamaki

I did not discover the power of travel until I was in my forties, when I took my first trip out of the United States. I was part of a project to create a sister city relationship with a small town in Japan, and I had the opportunity to be a part of the inaugural trip where the agreement to establish the relationship was signed. That was my first exposure to the strange sounds, smells, and tastes of a place that was truly foreign. Even a visit to a local food market was an eye-opening adventure because there were only a few food items I recognized. The street signs were written using characters that were as incomprehensible as the spoken language. But the hospitality was amazing as was the work ethic I witnessed in the factories I visited. I learned the local high schools did not employ janitors because having the students maintain the cleanliness of the school was viewed as an essential part of the students' educational experience, a concept that would probably not be well-received here in the United States.

It was a revelation to me that people could live so differently from me and still have successful lives. The insights I gained on that visit and the many other travel adventures I have experienced since that trip to Japan could not have been gained by reading or watching documentaries. The popular author of travel guides, Rick Steves, describes travel as "life intensified." I agree. There is something uniquely immersive about travel that creates experiences that cannot be captured in any other way. When those experiences are shared with family members, bonds are created that last a lifetime.

My Father-Son Bonding Journeys

I did not want my sons to wait until they were forty years old to begin having these experiences. Of all the things I've ever done, I am proudest of my two sons. My travel experiences with both my sons are treasures for me, but especially so with Matt since I don't have him here to share new experiences. Matt and I took a two-week father-son trip to Japan when he was fifteen. It was just the two of us. With our rail pass, we traveled all over Southern Japan. Our last stop was Tokyo. Matt had studied the map of the city intently. The day we arrived there, he asked me if we could take a tour around the city with him as our guide. I agreed, and with Matt leading the way, we took subways and the trains for hours, eventually ending up back at our hotel. Looking back, I have the very distinct sense that Matt grew up some that day. Successfully navigating us around this massive city and finding his way back to our hotel without my help was a real accomplishment and huge confidence booster for him. The message I got from him was "I just did Tokyo. And if I can do Tokyo, I can do anything."

I think we discover things about our children when we travel that we might not learn any other way. When I took my younger son Jonathan on his father-son trek, we decided to hike up the Schilthorn, the mountain in Switzerland that was featured in Her Majesty's Secret Service, an old James Bond movie. It was late in the day and I was exhausted as we reached a saddle of the mountain, not far from the summit. There was a gondola passing overhead taking people up to the mountaintop restaurant, our destination.

My son and I looked up toward the top, and while the distance was not great, it was very clear the trail was going to be very difficult and somewhat dangerous. It ran along a rugged cliff for maybe a quarter of a mile. From where we sat, we could see people inching their way along this segment of the trail, carefully holding onto a cable the Swiss had thoughtfully provided to prevent hikers from falling into the abyss below. When we looked the other direction, we could see a gondola stop—an easy, almost level walk where we could catch the gondola and ride the rest of the way up. So, there we were—we could take the easy route, or we could take the difficult route to the top as we had planned. What to do? After a long moment of reflection, my son looked at me and said, "Dad, we have to finish what we started, or we will always think of ourselves as quitters." This was one of those moments for me when, even then, I thought I should make a diary entry.

It's hard to know how much these experiences, or any experience, impacted my sons' lives when they became adults. I know for me, the quality time I had with them while exploring the world has been the best investment of both time and money I have ever made. The sounds, tastes, smells, and three-dimensional unfamiliarity of a different place creates the opportunity for shared personal discovery and growth that lasts a lifetime.

It's About the Time You Spend, Not the Distance You Travel

You don't have to venture to a foreign country to create quality experiences. They can come from the undistracted time you spend together, away from your ordinary life. Jenny Rosenstrach, author of the book *How to Celebrate Everything*, talks about a tradition she borrowed from a friend in which her husband celebrates each child's sixth birthday by taking that child on a weekend travel experience. They call it "Your

Wish Is My Command." Jenny's husband would hand the child a map and have them identify the places they could visit on a weekend trek. Whatever the child wanted to do, they did. It could be visiting a museum or swimming in a hotel pool. Jenny says each child and her husband can still recall every detail of the trip years later. They have now extended this idea to family vacations by having one parent spend an entire day with one of their children.

Rediscover Your Personal History

There is something deep within us that compels us to connect with where we came from. The American television miniseries based on Alex Haley's 1976 novel *Roots: The Saga of an American Family* won nine Primetime Emmy Awards and the final episode still holds a record as the second-most watched series finale in U.S. television history.

Most Americans have a personal history that can be traced back to another continent—Europe, Africa, or Asia. When we do the work to learn about those ancestors, we are often inspired by their bravery, struggle, and passion. Nothing galvanizes that connection quite like a visit to the villages they chose to leave to make the journey to the New World.

From La Rochelle to Quebec

My business partner, Robbie Trudeau, described the emotions she experienced when she visited La Rochelle, France and found a historical monument listing the name of her French ancestor, Etienne Trudeau, who left his village to make a life in Quebec. Robbie told me that she "... experienced the feeling of happiness, excitement, and freedom. I knew that Etienne had to work for five years without pay once he got to Quebec to pay for his passage. It was a kind of slavery. I thought, 'How amazing! Etienne was the forbearer of two Canadian Prime Ministers.'"

Visiting the Homeland of the Holocaust

For American Jews, visiting the homeland of family members who were killed in concentration camps can be an intense and enigmatic experience. In 2017, my friends Beverly Marshall and Steve Solomon visited Lithuania and Poland, in each place connecting with the grave markers of family members who had suffered persecution by Nazi Germany. Beverly's parents escaped the horror, but many of her close relatives did not. Beverly's great-grandmother, Laja Kempinska, died in 1931, before the German invasion, and was buried in the largest Jewish cemetery in Lodz. Beverly found some information about her, but not a complete record. She also found the burial site, but there was no headstone.

Beverly was uncertain about how the present-day inhabitants of Poland and Lithuania feel about what happened then. Who was responsible, who was not? "It's so intangible," she said. "There's nothing to tell, but maybe that's the story. They took away anything they could hold onto. What is certain is that my being in the places where my family lived and walking down streets they walked made their history more palpable. The losses cut in two ways—the destruction of a living people and their centuries-old culture, and the loss of the people who never had the chance to be, because of the parents and children who were cut down, shattering millions of family lines. My mother had no cousins, aunts, or uncles. They were wiped away." Beverly went on to say, "I went to pay my respects because no one else could do it. I went there for my grandmother and mother who couldn't go back. It meant it a lot to me, and I felt I was there for them." Steve and Beverly's complete journal of their 2017 journey is included in the resource link to this chapter.

Travel Can Make the American Story Real

We can learn about the American Revolution by reading about it or watching documentaries, but that can't compare to a visit to Boston Harbor or Independence Hall in Philadelphia. We can recite the Gettysburg address, but the impact of reading about it pales with the emotional experience of visiting the Gettysburg battlefield. Learning civics in high school has merit, but a visit to your congressman's office on Capitol Hill or watching Congress in session takes the experience to a new level.

It is easy for younger generations to assume the freedom and prosperity they enjoy have always been present and will continue unabated into the future. It is helpful to have them understand that the life we enjoy today was not available to our ancestors even a few generations ago. It is also useful for them to see that a real price was paid to create and to preserve what they now may take for granted. I believe thoughtfully imagined travel can drive home that message in a way that is more powerful than any other.

One Day in Normandy

A few years ago, we decided to splurge on a spring break trip to Paris with our two sons. We thought of it as an investment in their education, since neither had ever been to Europe at that time. We spent one of those days in Normandy. Normandy is a peaceful and bucolic place today, but having just watched *Saving Private Ryan* again, the images of the terrifying assault on the beaches back in 1944 were still in our heads.

In the early spring, it's cold in Normandy. The beaches are mostly deserted, but the images of young American soldiers engaged in deadly assault were still there. The concrete German bunkers were still very much there too. The American Cemetery is just up the hill. It's on American soil— the French government deeded it to the American

Battle Monuments Commission. It's immaculately groomed—there's no blade of grass untended.

There are almost 10,000 Americans interred there. No one has to ask you to be respectful: the place commands it. We moved slowly and quietly through the rows of simple crosses and Stars of David. Each soldier's name, date of birth, and date of death is inscribed on one side. My sons found the grave of a soldier from our state, only a couple years older than they were at the time. I was tempted to make some speech about how precious our freedom is and how these guys paid for it with their lives. I soon realized I didn't have to—the power of the place said it better than I ever could.

Travel is Not a Luxury. It is a Necessity.

My wife and I have come to believe that travel is an essential element of personal growth. The insights gained from actually being in different, even strange, places cannot be replaced by reading about it or through any kind of online experience. When we connect with people who think differently, believe differently and eat differently than we do, we are changed. We grow. We are better able to interpret the world. We are also less frightened of it. We discover that people of all beliefs and colors are very much like us, and are almost always kind, generous, and open. If I could, I would make travel a requirement to receive an undergraduate degree from a college or university. Our belief in the power of travel is why my wife and I created a charitable foundation to honor the memory of our son Matt. Our mission is to use the funds of the foundation to pay for travel experiences for young adults who would not otherwise have that opportunity.

As I said before, my investment in travel with my sons is the best investment I have ever made. Consider designing travel experiences for your younger generation family members as an important component of your legacy plan.

★★★★★★★★★★

The links to travel resources I could list would be endless. I have only provided a few. There is a link to Jenny Rosenstrach's book "How to Celebrate Everything" in which she describes some travel traditions her family has developed for their young children. There are some other books listed, including a link to Rick Steves' travel guides. In my house, we call these books our "Ricky Books." Rick has helped me immerse myself in local culture in Europe more than once.

www.YourAmericanLegacy.com/resources

YOUR AMERICAN LEGACY

"Death is more universal than life. Everyone dies, but not everyone lives."

—ALAN SACHS

CHAPTER EIGHTEEN

Make Your Funeral a Teaching Moment

You Will Have Their Attention. Use it Wisely

" Talking about sex won't make you pregnant. Talking about death won't make you die." This is what author Gail Rubin tells us in her now famous Ted Talk. She makes the point that thinking about the inevitability of your passing should not be a taboo subject. The idea of using your death as an occasion to share your wisdom and life lessons is an opportunity that should not be wasted. The people who are most important in your life will be there. Their children, and perhaps their grandchildren, will also be there. For a few hours, you will be the focus of their attention. What would you like for them to take away from that experience that will be useful and lasting for them? Your funeral can be a powerful teaching moment.

I would expand this idea somewhat to say that your final days as well as your funeral are opportunities to demonstrate the values, life lessons and faith that matter most to you. When Pope John Paul II was in the last few days of his life, the Roman Catholic Church used his impending death as a demonstration of how to die in a way that was consistent with Catholic doctrine. More recently, Senator John McCain used the press coverage he knew his death would generate as an occasion to give voice to a political point of view that was important to him. Many people I know who disagreed with Senator McCain's politics nonetheless recognized how effective he was in using the media coverage surrounding his death to articulate his message.

Funerals Are More than Flowers and Sermons Now

The Baby Boomer generation has changed everything it has touched. When Boomers were in their twenties, they redefined popular music, grew long hair and marched in protest of the Vietnam war. Now, as they reach their seventies, they are redefining how to die. Funerals no longer must be the somber, traditional ceremonies they once were. These events have become an opportunity for a final creative expression of life.

In fact, some of these occasions are no longer funerals. These ceremonies are often referred to as "Celebrations of Life" and are held weeks or even months after the death occurs to provide time to properly plan and to give the people attending the ceremony the opportunity to make travel arrangements. In the same way that people hire wedding planners, final event planners now design and manage the ceremony and the social events surrounding the occasion of a person's passing. In the resource links to this chapter, we provide a number of examples of ways people are making funerals and life celebrations an imaginative experience. That creativity can serve a purpose—it can provide you a venue to tell the story of your struggles, wins, insights, and faith in ways that are uniquely compelling. It can have a lasting impact on the people that are important to you and perhaps others you don't even know.

Write Your Obituary

I have had the opportunity—if you can call it that—to write obituaries for close family members who died. I can tell you that, in the midst of grief, it is a challenge to face a blank computer screen and compose the words that will be the final coda to the life of someone you love. I encourage my clients to provide some assistance to the person tasked with this duty by creating a list of the major points they would like to have included. I provide my clients with an outline to make this process easier, and I have included that document in the resource materials accompanying this chapter. Going the additional step and writing it would be even better.

At one time, I encouraged only my older clients to outline or write their obituary. However, after reading Stephen Covey's book *The Seven Habits of Highly Successful People*, I changed my mind. In this book, the author makes the point that successful people "begin with the end in mind." Since our death and memorial event will define the end of our lives here on earth, Covey encourages us to imagine who will eulogize us and to take the additional step of putting that eulogy in writing. It is also a good idea to write the obituary you would like people to read about you. The eulogy and obituary he challenges us to write are not what would be published if we died tomorrow. It's the ones we would want to be read and published after we have accomplished the things we believe we were put here to accomplish.

Michael Hyatt and Daniel Harkavy say essentially the same thing in their book *Living Forward*. The exercise of writing the final words to be spoken about you can be galvanizing because it engages us fully with the reality that our time here is finite. While days may seem to pass from one to another in endless succession, this exercise connects us to the reality that there will be an end. It allows us to seize the power to define the meaning of the time we have been given.

It's Your Death. Take Control of it and Preserve the Peace

The impending death and final passing of a family member is an emotional time. When adult children are brought together to make end of life or funeral planning decisions, it is very common for childhood grievances to emerge. Do we discontinue life support or keep mom on a ventilator and give her another chance to recover? Do we buy this expensive casket or this more ordinary one? Do we cremate our loved one to save even more money? These are the kinds of decisions that provide an occasion for ancient hostilities to emerge. One of the important goals of almost all my clients is to preserve family harmony. The more of these decisions you make, the fewer opportunities your family will have to create rifts that can last for years or even a lifetime.

Make Your End of Life Health Care Choices Clear

In addition to thoughtfully planning your final arrangements, I strongly encourage you to sign a medical power of attorney designating the person or persons that you choose to give the authority to make life and death (as well as other care) decisions if you are unable to make them for yourself. Name a sequence of persons in case the first person you name is unavailable. If you want more than one person to work together to make these decisions, you can say that in the legal document. Two companion documents need to be signed as well—a living will that outlines your general desires about the termination of life support in the event there is a general consensus that you will not recover from the illness and a HIPPA document that names the people who will have access to your medical information and have consent to be present when there are meetings with your doctors. The people you name in your HIPPA form (other than your health care agent) will not have the authority to make decisions on your behalf, but they will be able to be in the room, hear the medical explanations of your condition, and offer opinions that your health care agent may consider or ignore. It is awkward and divisive to have people who care about you excluded from these conversations.

I also recommend that you make a point, while you are fully alert, to have a discussion with the persons you designated as your health care agents to inform them of your general thinking about what kind of decisions you would want them to make. I encourage you to not be too specific. For example, my experience has shown that an absolute mandate such as "never put me on a ventilator" is a bad idea. Sometimes, these devices do what they were designed to do, and patients really do recover.

My recommendation is that you provide your health care agents with clear general guidance about the outcomes you want—such as not being kept alive by artificial means for any period of time—and trust them to use their best judgment to consult with your medical team about the details. If you want to be an organ donor (or if you don't), you should make your intentions clear. I can say from personal experience that it is a very tough decision to make someone an organ donor when you have no idea if that is what they would have wanted. When you are clear about what you want, and your family knows you have made your intentions known, it removes a massive amount of potential guilt around the decision-making process. It also gives your health care agent a way to explain their decisions to other family members who may disagree with the choices they make. Nailing down the health care decisions is one important step to assuring family harmony after you are gone.

Pre-Arrange Your Final Services

Finally, I suggest that you also consider pre-arranging the basics of your final services. You can choose the mortuary where the final arrangements will be handled and decide whether you will be buried or cremated as well as design other details of the service. You can also lock in the cost of the arrangements today so that future inflation will not impact the cost of your burial or cremation. By making these decisions, you remove one of the most significant flashpoints in family relationships that arise in the hours and days following your death. It's also worth noting that prepaying your funeral arrangements is a permitted expenditure that can speed up your qualification for receiving Medicaid benefits if you need nursing home care.

Family Unity is the Best Legacy

Making your end of life health care choices clear and planning the basics of your final arrangements are valuable gifts you can give to your family. With these decisions made, they can spend their time remembering and sharing stories about you and reflecting on the wisdom and meaning you have added to their lives. If they choose, they can also plan additional events to celebrate your life. Your passing can be an occasion that builds family unity. It can also be an occasion for you to share important life lessons with younger generation family members. Family unity is the best legacy—it's worth the modest investment required to ensure unity is preserved.

★★★★★★★★★★

In the resources to this chapter, I have provided a link to Gail Rubin's famous Ted Talk "A Good Goodbye: Funeral Planning for Those Who Don't Plan to Die." You will also find a link to Stephen Covey's best-selling book The Seven Habits of Highly Effective People. *One of the seven habits Covey identifies is the habit of "Beginning with the End in Mind." I have also provided a link to* Living Forward *by Michael Hyatt and Daniel Harkavy as well as some other resources.*

www.YourAmericanLegacy.com/resources

YOUR AMERICAN LEGACY

"The biggest problem is we do not listen to understand. We listen to reply."

—PETER DRUCKER

CHAPTER NINETEEN

Break Through Communication Barriers with Powerful New Communication Strategies

The Parents Story

The parents sat in my conference room in silence. The wife was sobbing. "Help me understand what happened," I finally asked. It was difficult for me to extract the story from them.

"Our daughter got married about six months ago," the woman finally began. "I don't know what we did. I really don't. It just seems like her husband has decided he doesn't want to have anything to do with us. He has just totally alienated our daughter from us. She won't return my calls. She won't respond to my texts. I'm afraid to go to her house. I'm afraid her husband will call the police. I don't know what we've done. We were always so close. We shared everything. She was my best friend."

The husband, holding back his own tears, said in almost a whisper, "I guess you'd say our hearts are broken. I really think that's why I'm seeing a cardiologist. We've worked all our lives and saved to have what we have. I can't imagine leaving it to someone that won't speak to us. We want to change our trust so that she gets exactly zero. That's why we're here." I handed out tissue as I gathered the details of how this once close relationship had disintegrated into estrangement.

Estate planning attorneys have conversations much like this one with uncommon frequency. These estrangements can last for years or even a lifetime and impair the ability of the grandparents to know and spend time with their grandchildren. They often occur in situations when stress is heightened—when life and death health decisions are being made for an ill or aging parent, for example. These divisions also happen after the death of a parent when the estate is being settled and the assets, especially family heirlooms, are being divided.

When divisions in families happen, I have found that it is rare that anyone committed any act that we would describe as dishonest or criminal to cause the breakdown in the relationship. These breakdowns are usually caused by small but hurtful things that have spiraled out of control. In the moment of hurt or anger, the damage seems irreparable, and the possibility of having a meaningful relationship seems truly impossible. One of the benefits of being an estate planner is that we have the benefit of perspective, and that perspective has taught me that these estrangements are often temporary if the right steps are taken. I also know that, in most cases, the deep hurt and anger that results from these estrangements can be repaired or prevented.

Three Action Steps

The legacy of a positive, loving relationship between family members is important, and I do not believe they are accidental. While every family will have divisions and estrangements from time to time, there is a lot we can do to influence the quality of those relationships. In this chapter, I will focus on the importance of developing healthy communication strategies for the obvious reason that the health of our relationships with each other is determined by our ability to understand and communicate with each other. The ability to instill our legacy in younger generation family members first requires that we have a positive, meaningful relationship with those family members.

In the discussion that follows, I outline three specific action steps you can take that will immediately improve the quality of family communication. The resources at the end of this chapter will allow you to take a deeper dive into family communication strategies.

Action Step Number One: Appreciate Our Differences

We are all wired differently and experience the world differently. This may seem obvious, but I think it's common for us to lose sight of that. When we do, we become frustrated and even angry that others don't see or experience things in the same way we do.

I recently spent the day with a client family who was experiencing deep conflict. To make matters worse, the mother and son were in business together. The conflict was about to erupt into litigation if the differences could not be resolved. I listened for several hours to what they both had to say. At a point well into the conversation, a light came on for me, and I saw clearly what was happening. They both loved each other deeply but had no idea what each needed from the other. The mother had created several business opportunities that had turned out to be financially successful and had gifted them to her son. She was angry that he did not appreciate all she had done for him.

The son, it turned out, was angry that his mother had given him anything. At one point he said through tears, "I've never wanted you to give me anything. Since I was nine years old, I've wanted to earn everything I have!" There it was, laid bare, but neither of them could see it—they were each trying to give something to the other they thought the other wanted and hoped to receive love in return. The mother couldn't understand why the son didn't appreciate her generous gifts. The son couldn't understand why his mother didn't appreciate his flinty self-reliance. They were just wired differently.

There are several personality tests that can help you get a deeper insight into those differences. I use the DISC test before we hire any new employee in our firm, partly to see if their personality is a fit for the position, and partly to improve communication among our team members. I am convinced that if each team member understands the unique personality profile of the other team members, they will be more appreciative and hopefully more tolerant of each other.

This DISC test can be used the same way in families. It can be taken online in about twenty minutes. By answering about thirty seemingly innocuous questions, it's possible to learn the personality traits of an individual with remarkable accuracy. I also like and use the KOLBE test which can also be taken online. Most people I know who have taken either of these tests or other tests, such as the Meyers-Briggs, are quite stunned by how accurately the results describe themselves. I encourage families to choose one of these tests and have every family member take it. It will give each family member insight into the other family members and help everyone better understand that much of individual behavior, and especially communication patterns, is baked into the very nature of the person. Knowing that opens the door to mutual understanding.

Action Step Number Two: Understand the Story Spiral

Fractures in family relationships almost always begin with a story, and by the time the fracture has become emotional, there are several chapters to it. The book *Crucial Conversations, Tools for Talking When Stakes are High* describes these stories as "spirals." The authors of this book are often brought in as consultants to resolve conflicts that appear beyond repair. They challenge the individuals in conflict to retrace the steps of the story back to its source. Each person moves from their emotional reaction back to what he or she concluded and then further back to what he or she observed. That process takes each participant back to the place where the conflict began and where their feelings can be resolved. I have observed this process up close and have witnessed broken relationships restored. It works when each participant is willing to listen to the other person describe the steps in the spiral.

Action Step Number Three:
Proactively Communicate

Saying things, not just thinking them, is powerful. During World War II,
President Roosevelt regularly held live "Fireside Chats" over the radio
because he knew that Americans needed to be comforted and reassured.
Winston Churchill reassured Britons in the same way as London was
on the receiving end of nightly bombing raids. President Reagan went
to Berlin and, in front of thousands of Germans, called on President
Gorbachev to "Tear down this wall!" Good leaders know they can't sit
in their office and just think these thoughts. These thoughts must be
expressed so the intended audience can hear them and be impacted by
them. Marriages can legally be done with some paperwork and a justice of
the peace, and public officials could take office without a public swearing-
in. But we know intuitively that commitments that matter need to be
spoken aloud, and sometimes in the presence of witnesses.

Personal relationships are no different. Important things need to be said,
not implied or assumed. Some people need connection and reassurance
more than others. I know people who are entirely self-contained. They
don't need external validation. If you're wired like that, it may be difficult
for you to appreciate how much other people who do have that need rely
on your affirmation. Appreciating what the people you care about need to
hear from you is an important aspect of creating and nurturing successful
and satisfying relationships. If they need to hear "I love you" from you, then
just say it. Don't make them beg for it. Say it generously and often.

Too much goes unsaid between people who care about each other. We
never know for sure if we have tomorrow to say these things, so the right
time to say them is today. Say them as often as you can and in as many
ways as you can. When I am on a business trip, my wife becomes irritated
when I don't call her. "I've been busy and don't have anything to say," I
tell her. She responds, "It doesn't matter; I want to hear your voice." I get
it. We need to proactively reach out even when we don't have anything
of importance to say. Just reaching out with a phone call, text, email or

handwritten note tells that person they are being thought about and that they matter. I know that these calls, notes, and texts all serve as deposits in a goodwill account you may need to draw on when a conflict does arise.

Two American Presidents, Bill Clinton and the late George H. W. Bush, both known for having exceptional people skills, are also known as legendary note writers. Bush consistently produced about twenty-five personal notes every day, usually plunked out on an old manual typewriter. Clinton started writing notes early in his career. My business partner Bill Conway recalled for me the handwritten note he received from Clinton thanking him for his help after a failed student government campaign at Georgetown University. For both Bush and Clinton, the connections they made and nurtured with a disciplined, proactive personal outreach give us insight into their mindset and go a long way in explaining their political success. Their success can be instructional for all of us. If note-writing can advance a political career, it can also work to create and preserve family harmony.

If Tiger Woods Needs a Golf Coach...

We all know that Tiger Woods is one of the most successful golfers in the world. What you may not know is that Tiger frequently hires a golf coach when he thinks his swing or short game needs some work. Many top professional athletes hire personal coaches. It's also very common now for successful business owners to hire coaches or participate with other business owners in coaching or peer group programs.

If successful people in sports and business find value in coaching, doesn't it make sense for us to reach out for advice to help us improve the relationships that are important to us? A professional counsellor can help us resolve conflicts and improve our communication skills. That outside perspective, coming from someone who is not emotionally involved in the conflict can make all the difference. The investment you make in relationship coaching—or counseling—is an investment in the quality of your life and the lives of your family members. I frequently encourage my clients to seek counseling, either from a professional therapist, minister or staff member at their church, synagogue or mosque. Reaching out for help is a sign of strength, not weakness. It's what the most successful professionals and business owners do.

Family Meetings

One of the best tools to strengthen family bonds and improve communication is a regular family meeting. Ideally this would be a weekly meeting. The families that do this often have their meetings at regular times, usually at the end of the week, and they have an agenda. Family meetings only need to last twenty minutes, but that's enough time to find out what worked and what didn't work during the week and to plan for the week ahead. This meeting creates a venue where the entire family can be engaged in solving problems. It reduces stress and builds solidarity while reinforcing family culture and values. Children learn valuable life skills just by participating in these meetings. I have provided some links to resources that offer ideas for how to make family meetings productive and enjoyable.

Publish Family Newsletters

When families become larger and more dispersed around the country or the world, a newsletter can be an effective tool to keep the family connected. These can be printed and mailed or shared by e-mail. I have provided some resources that show examples of great family newsletters along with some advice on how to create yours. An alternative to a newsletter format is a private family Facebook page. Facebook will allow you to create a page that provides a venue for families to share ongoing communication with each other that is only available to members of the family. Large, dispersed families need tools like these to efficiently keep the family connected.

Now More than Ever, Grandparents, Aunts and Uncles Matter

Because it's common now for grandparents to live hundreds or even thousands of miles from their grandchildren, it is more important than ever to underscore the importance of the role grandparents have in their lives. Author Alex Haley put it this way: "Nobody can do for little children what grandparents do. Grandparents sort of sprinkle stardust over the lives of little children." Grandparents are an anchor in a turbulent sea of change. Sociologists have found that children who have a high-level of grandparent involvement have fewer emotional and behavioral problems.

Grandparents are the family connection to the past. Their personal history is their grandchildren's link to their own identity. Connecting grandchildren to their roots provides the connection that renews the meaning of family. With the help of technology, this can be done, even if you live far away. Most of my clients who are grandparents are active on Facebook, and their primary reason is to stay connected to their grandchildren.

Grandparents can also travel with their grandchildren. They can take them to destinations that correlate with places or events they are studying in school. They can volunteer with them and give them a direct experience of personal generosity. In chapter twenty-one, I describe how family charitable foundations or donor advised funds can be easily created, even with modest financial contributions. I encourage my clients to create these as a tool to teach generosity to younger family members. Grandparents can be particularly useful in this activity by helping their grandchildren research charities and suggest causes they would like to support.

The most powerful thing grandparents can do, however, is to continually communicate positive messages of love and affirmation. These messages can be communicated verbally and in writing. Here are some examples of words grandchildren need to hear:

> I like you just the way you are.
>
> I love spending time with you.
>
> Nothing you do will ever make me stop loving you.

You don't have to do anything to earn my love.

You can be proud of your heritage: I will tell you about it.

Aunts and uncles can play that same role in the lives of their nieces and nephews. When grandchildren, nieces and nephews absorb these messages, the impact will be lasting. It will provide stability and security as they grow into adults.

Lasting, Caring Relationships Are Worth the Effort

The time we spend understanding our differences and proactively working to prevent or to resolve family conflicts with patience and love is definitely worth the effort.

Several months after the conversation I described at the opening of this chapter, I received a phone call from my client. "Guess who is coming to Thanksgiving dinner?" he asked. Before I could answer, he said, "We resolved things with our daughter. We want to revise our trust again. We want to put her back in." Reconciliation happens.

★★★★★★★★★★★

My team and I have provided an extensive collection of resources here that will be useful in improving the quality of family communication. You will find a link to Crucial Conversations, which I have personally found to be a particularly effective tool. You will also find links to websites that make it easy to take online personality tests (something I believe is truly useful) as well as links to several Ted Talks we like. There are links to some books, some focused specifically on the important role of grandparents.

www.YourAmericanLegacy.com/resources

YOUR AMERICAN LEGACY

"We make a living by what we get, but we make a life by what we give."

—WINSTON CHURCHILL

CHAPTER TWENTY

Harness the Power of Generosity

Theresa's Story

The moment Theresa Russo was born her parents knew something was wrong. Theresa was diagnosed with microcephaly, a birth defect the doctors said would preclude her from ever having a normal life. Her condition was so severe that her parents were told she would likely never leave the hospital.

Theresa did go home and lived until the age of five. When she passed, the Russo family decided to do something special to honor her memory and the inspiration she had given them. They formed The Theresa Foundation which funds the Theresa Academy of Performing Arts in Long Island, New York, a bright, positive space where children with special needs can spend their days expressing themselves through dance, singing, puppet-making, and dozens of other creative activities. The center is an inspiring place—a model of how children with special needs can be challenged to live beyond the limits most people assume they have.

The Theresa Foundation is a project that has engaged the passion of the entire Russo family. The Russo children are all adults now and work in different parts of the country, but their commitment to The Theresa Foundation keeps them connected with the shared purpose of improving and expanding the lives of these children with special needs.

The impact of losing a child or a sibling is unexplainably profound. Transforming that loss into something positive in the lives of others is a powerful act of generosity. Theresa Russo has been gone for more than twenty years now, but she continues to influence the Russo family in positive ways. Generosity is an incredibly powerful thing: it can work magic in the world and in the life of your family.

A Generosity Mindset Has Transformative Power

Purposeful acts of generosity have transformative power. In his book *"Beating the Midas Curse,"* Rod Zeeb uses the term "Transformational Philanthropy" to describe the concept that a gift has as profound an impact on the donor as it does on the person receiving it. He also points out that the transformation that takes place has little to do with the size of the gift, but instead reflects the passion behind it. My personal experience confirms this truth.

Every major religion recognizes the value and power of generosity. In Buddhism, practicing generosity is understood as a way to train the mind that leads to attaining enlightenment. Giving serves to eliminate one's greed and ill will. In Islam, the concept of generosity is so central that it is embedded in one of the five core pillars of the religion. One of the most familiar and enigmatic quotations attributed directly to Jesus in the Christian New Testament—expressed in slightly different ways in each of the four gospels—is this: "If you want to gain your life, you must lose it." This expresses a fundamental principle that goes to the core of how human beings are designed to function in the world, and I understand it to mean that if you want to live a joyful life, you must invest it in service to others.

The wisdom of that insight is certainly validated in my personal experience. There have been those times when I found myself in a self-absorbed funk, and the only solution that worked to break me out of it was to find a way to invest myself emotionally in an outwardly focused act of generosity of some kind. I'm not unique in this. I have noticed that my happiest clients and friends are the people that are the most generous. Self-absorbed and miserly people are not fun to be around, and I suspect they don't enjoy being alone with themselves much either.

What Do Generosity and Eating Chocolate Have in Common?

In the resource materials for this chapter, we provide a link to a research project that establishes that when we engage in selfless acts of giving, our brain responds in a similar way to eating chocolate. When we give, the portion of our brain that is responsible for our cravings and pleasure rewards lights up. A 2011 study at the University of Notre Dame also found that the practice of generosity was a key factor in marital happiness and a significant factor in reducing the likelihood of divorce.

The generosity impulse emerges early. A research project conducted by psychologists at the University of British Columbia in Vancouver found solid evidence that toddlers were clearly happier when they engaged in "painful generosity." In their experiment, these psychologists found that toddlers were significantly happier when they shared their treats than they were when they kept all the treats that were given to them. People achieve a greater level of fulfillment when they are working on something bigger than themselves, especially when that something is about more than just money. Reconnecting with our innate sense of generosity is positive and healthy for us, and teaching our younger generation family members to connect with theirs can be transformative for them.

It's a Dog-Eat-Dog World...Or Is It?

In their book *The Go-Giver*, authors Bob Berg and John David Mann describe conventional wisdom we all know and understand. To be successful, we have to recognize that it's a dog eat dog world. To win in the competitions of life, it is necessary to be hard-nosed negotiators and cut the sharpest deals. If we're tough, we can extract the maximum advantage and gain the most benefit for ourselves. If we don't get that advantage, our competitors will, and we will be left to starve. However, these authors go on to say that while things do often appear to be that way on the surface, when we look deeper, they are not like that at all. It turns out the universe is a friendly place, designed from creation to reward authentic generosity.

A Spontaneous Gift Turns into More

When I was a young lawyer, my client acquired a company on the East Coast and he asked me to help with the ownership transition. Late one night, he and I were flying home when he decided to share a story about something seemingly very ordinary. He told me how he walked into the dining hall of the business he had acquired and—knowing that the woman working the cash register was the wife of the pastor of a small church in the area—he impulsively signed over his travel reimbursement check to her with instructions to give the check to her husband's church. The check was for $500.

He then told me that within a month of his having made that spontaneous gift, a customer who had an unpaid account he thought was uncollectable walked in and paid it off. The amount the customer owed was $50,000. He told me these stories because he was certain they were connected. He believed that because he had spontaneously given the pastor's wife $500, he was rewarded by receiving $50,000 he was sure he would never collect. He explained to me that this is how the universe works—when you give generously without expecting anything in return, you are always rewarded. "Stan, you can't give and expect something in return," he said. "You have to give without expecting anything in return." I knew this client and his family well. He lived his life that way. He moved through life with the joyful, childlike trust that the universe was hard-wired for generosity.

I believe Berg and Mann have it right. In moments of stillness, we may become aware of a presence that is larger than ourselves and inextricably connected to the deeper part of us. I believe that presence is divine, eternal, and larger than I will ever be able to comprehend. I also know that it is generous. If we learn to trust that presence and open ourselves to the abundance and generosity that is available to us, every aspect of our lives will be infused with confidence and power that far exceeds what is possible when we compete alone and from a place of scarcity. I know this sounds very spiritual, and I suppose it is. But my experience, and the experience of the most successful people I know, validates this underlying truth of the universe.

Because this understanding of how things work is so counter-intuitive to conventional wisdom, it is not always easy to trust our best instincts and allow a mindset of generosity to guide our attitude and decisions. But with repeated experiences, we can grow to a place where generosity and abundance become the attitudes that govern our lives. The strategies we outline in this chapter can be effective in teaching younger generation family members that the universe is truly an abundant and generous place. By allowing an attitude of authentic generosity to shape their personal and financial lives, it will also allow them to experience more joy, fulfillment, and, perhaps surprisingly, greater financial success.

Generosity is the Antidote to Affluenza

Most of my clients are regular middle-class folks, but I do have some who have done rather well for themselves. Almost all my wealthy clients have what we call "first generation" wealth. They started with very little and now, decades later, do not think of themselves as wealthy. They do not live the kind of lifestyle typically associated with wealth. I know their stories well enough to know their wealth was created through risk-taking, grit, and real work. Usually their children, the people I call the "second generation," are old enough to have memories of the struggle that went into the creation of their parents' wealth and retain an appreciation for the commitment and sacrifice the first generation made to build it. But by the time the "third generation" arrives on the scene, however, the family has usually been comfortable for decades, and the first generation may even be gone.

Usually, the third generation and the generations beyond it have lost their connection to the source of the wealth. While they did nothing to help create it, they're quite willing to spend it and enjoy the status it brings. In my experience, the life experience of the third generation and the generations that come after are so different from that of the first generation that relating to each other is difficult. It's not uncommon for the first and second generations to be aware of this shift in mindset, so they seek me out to find ways to reconnect the younger generations with the values that created their financial security. I often hear my clients express horror at the thought they worked their entire lives to create wealth only to have it consumed by ungrateful heirs who don't work, don't contribute to their community, and spend their inheritance on drugs, alcohol, and frivolous living. I think their point is very well taken.

As Baby Boomers retire and die, the number of people who will receive wealth they did not create themselves will accelerate dramatically over the next thirty years. Even the most conservative estimates say that thirty trillion dollars in wealth will pass to a generation that did not earn it. If we don't manage this transition well, the consequences will not bode well for the heirs that inherit this wealth, and it will not bode well for the future of the country. When wealth is wisely managed and invested, it can be a power tool for the financial security of future generations and a healthy, growing economy. When wealth is wasted, it undermines the very foundations of our democracy. We have an obligation to future generations to get this right.

A purposeful generosity plan is an essential part of a comprehensive strategy in producing a well-adjusted and responsible next generation. I believe affluenza can be avoided by helping younger generation family members develop a healthy relationship to wealth. An intentional generosity plan is a key part of that education. If you want well-grounded, happy children, grandchildren, nieces and nephews, then help them discover the power of personal generosity. Learning to internalize a generosity mindset is as important as learning reading, writing, math or science. Children who make generosity a part of their lives are happier, healthier, and more productive.

Update How You Think About Giving

Most of us associate the word "philanthropy" with billionaires funding foundations, colleges or a cancer treatment center at the medical school. In his book *Giving: Purpose is the New Currency*, Alexandre Mars challenges us to think about giving differently—as something we should all be doing consistently and systematically. "Sharing needs to become transformational and natural: a way of life that will bring us back together. This is about everyday people choosing to change the way they think about giving, not billionaires donating millions." He encourages employers, for example, to set up giving programs through payroll deduction in the same way they offer 401(k) programs, including employer matching. He challenges each of us to find a level of giving that is painless. Giving, he says, should "… always bring happiness, not only to the recipient but to the giver as well." Mars recognizes that the reluctance to give often arises out of a lack of trust of charities and a lack of knowledge of what giving opportunities are available. After creating his personal fortune in several tech start-ups, Mars formed the Epic Foundation to provide an independent, objective team operating globally to identify the non-profit organizations that have the potential to make the greatest impact while also operating efficiently and ethically. Nonprofit watchdogs like Charity Navigator and Guidestar also provide an independent source of information on the efficiency and effectiveness of not-for-profit organizations. Imagine the impact we would have on poverty, hunger and abuse in the world if all of us made the decision to give painless amounts to well-run not-for-profit organizations every month.

What do You Have to Give? It's More than Money

You may have noticed that I have used the word "generosity" in this chapter rather than the word "philanthropy." I have generally avoided the word "philanthropy" because that term usually conjures up the idea we should be reaching for our checkbooks. Don't misunderstand me—I fully support philanthropy. Without it, critical charitable work couldn't be done. Hospitals, religious institutions, and universities would have to close their doors. But "generosity" is a bigger concept and involves more than simply giving money away.

In his book *Connected for Good*, author John Stanley challenges us to reimagine the way we think about generosity in our lives so that we are no longer motivated to give out of a sense of guilt or obligation. Rather, he encourages us to give from our heart's desire for connection to others and a passion for creating change in the world. He makes a compelling argument that we humans are hard-wired for connection. We are happier and healthier, and the world is a better place when we operate as part of a community.

When generosity emerges out of our innate desire for connection and a passion for making a difference, it becomes possible for us to then assess all the resources we have that can empower connection. Those resources extend far beyond the money we have in the bank to include the skills we have, the connections we can make between people, the ability to listen intently, possessions we no longer need, and perhaps a spare room in our home or a vacation home we use only occasionally. I am quite confident that everyone has something of value that can be useful to others. A thoughtful generosity plan recognizes the uniqueness of what we have to offer and creates the opportunity for each of us to give whatever we have to give.

Friday Nights at the Ranch

Rodger Johnson is a successful financial advisor in Tyler, Texas. He and his wife Crystal remain very close to their adult children. A few years ago, he decided to become more encouraging in helping his children to develop a passion for making a difference in their community. In their regular Friday night family dinners at the ranch, Rodger began making cash gifts to each of the four children and prompting discussion about how they planned to use these gifts to make a difference. Rodger tells me that his children have become much more aware of the needs of those around them and are more engaged in reaching out to meet those needs. He also tells me that the Friday night dinner conversations with his children are much more interesting and rewarding. This approach to generosity is not complicated and does not require a lawyer or a large financial investment. What it does require is intentionality and thoughtfulness.

Noted Auburn professor Kalu Ndukwe Kalu spoke to the power of generosity in this simple expression:

"The things you do for yourself are gone when you are gone
but the things you do for others remain as your legacy."

Many of my firm's clients are retirees who moved south to escape the cold winters in the upper Midwest. It's always interesting for me to talk to them when they first arrive. They tell me they are tired of working and looking forward to spending the rest of their lives playing golf and fishing. When I talk to them six months later, I ask how their golf game is going. Generally, they'll say, "Oh, I still golf a couple times a week, but I'm volunteering at the local high school now, and I'm on the board of the Boy Scouts. I got bored just golfing. I'm having a lot more fun with these kids." One of America's most famous rabbis had this to say about how engaging in acts of generosity makes you feel:

"Caring about others, leaving an impact on people, brings happiness. When you carry out acts of kindness you get a wonderful feeling inside. It is as though something inside your body responds and says, yes, this is how I ought to feel"

—RABBI HAROLD KUSHNER

Like the Rabbi said—we're hard-wired for generosity.

★★★★★★★★★★

In the resource links to this chapter, you will find references to several helpful books as well as the links to the Teresa Foundation,

www.YourAmericanLegacy.com/resources

YOUR AMERICAN LEGACY

"No one has ever become poor by giving."

—ANNE FRANK

CHAPTER TWENTY-ONE

Get the Most Value Out of Your Giving

How Cutting Firewood and Charitable Giving Are Related

A friend of mine once told me that it was always good to cut your own firewood. "It warms you twice," he said. When clients are open to the idea of making charitable contributions, either during their lifetime or as a part of their estate plan at death, their first thought is usually to provide me with the list of charitable causes that matter to them. Quite often, it is their church or a local hospital. That kind of giving is important. Churches, synagogues, mosques, and art museums rely on consistent, predictable contributions to create a budget, pay staff, keep the lights on, and provide programming.

So while I fully support direct charitable giving, I do point out that the benefits of giving can be multiplied if is implemented through a family charitable entity. If you make your gift directly to a charity, the charity then has the money and can use it to accomplish positive charitable purposes. Following my friend's thinking about firewood, that gift "warms you once."

However, if you make the same gift through your family charitable entity, you can engage your children and grandchildren in a thoughtful discussion about how this contribution can be used to make a positive difference in the world. Your contribution to your family charitable entity will ultimately go to a charitable cause because it legally has to, and it could be the same charities you would have given the contribution to if you had made the contribution directly. But by engaging your younger generation family members in the decision-making process, you connect with them in a way that is potentially transformative for them. This may prompt them to discover their own passion to make a difference.

For this strategy to work, it is essential to allow these younger generation family members some creative flexibility to influence the direction of the gifts. It will not work if you expect them to simply rubber-stamp your directives. If you open the door and allow the creative engagement of your younger generation family members, the secondary benefit resulting from that engagement may be more valuable over time than your monetary contribution. Understood in that way, the contribution to your family charitable entity "warms you twice."

Creating a Family Charity is Easier Than You Think

Charitable entities can be created in a variety of forms. The right format for your family depends on your specific objectives, the role you want your family members to play in its operation and the amount you plan to contribute to it, either now or later.

The simplest and least expensive way to create a family charity is to establish a donor-advised fund at your local community foundation or your religious denomination's charitable foundation. A donor-advised fund (or DAF) is created with a simple agreement between you and the charity defining your charitable goals, and the names of the initial advisors who will make recommendations to the charity on how distributions are to be made. This fund is called "donor-advised" because the advisors only make recommendations on distributions—they do not have actual control over them. However, I have found that community foundations will follow the recommendations of the fund's advisors if they are legal and comply with the overall mission of the fund as expressed in the agreement. While the community foundation that manages the DAF does not typically charge a fee to establish it, they will charge the fund a fee each year to cover the operating overhead of the foundation. In my experience, these fees are quite reasonable. A DAF can be created with contributions as small as $5000. This is the most painless and trouble-free way to create a family charity. It allows you to focus your effort entirely on gifting while the community foundation manages the tax reporting and legal compliance work.

If greater control over the entity is important to you, you will want to consider creating a private family foundation. This version of a family charity allows family members to be compensated for the work they do for the foundation. It also allows the family to retain complete control over investment decisions and charitable distributions. However, because of the potential for abuse, the IRS has imposed regulations governing the operation of private family foundations that require minimum annual distributions be made from the foundation. A DAF, however, can decide to not make a charitable distribution in a particular year. This decision might make sense if the value of the investment portfolio has suffered in a down market, but a private foundation doesn't have that flexibility.

There are costs associated with creating a private foundation and obtaining its tax-exempt status as well as costs to manage the tax and other reporting requirements annually. There are other restrictions that might make a private foundation an inappropriate choice for your family. However, a private foundation may be a good choice for families that want control and who are willing to contribute a few hundred thousand dollars or more to the foundation.

Private foundations can be created in a variety of legal formats. There are also hybrid versions of family charities such as supporting organizations (SOs) that blend some of the benefits of public charities with the opportunity for deeper family involvement in management. It is important to have a professional who understands charitable planning options outline the pros and cons of the available choices.

Build Traditions around Your Foundation

A family charitable entity can be a powerful, long-term strategy to preserve and enhance the family brand and grow younger generation family members into healthy, contributing adults. I encourage our clients to create the foundation and fund it while they are living rather than wait and have the organization created upon their death. If you create it now, you'll have the opportunity to infuse it with your own passion. You can begin to establish the traditions you will want continued after you are gone. If you are thinking long-term, having the organization already created and operating provides your adult children with an existing structure and traditions, so the path for bringing their children into the charitable process is already established for them.

Whatever legal form it takes, your family charity will be a far more effective tool over time if you build an emotional connection around its operation. I believe this is the key to your charity's long-term success. I explored the power of ritual and ceremony in Chapter Sixteen, but here I make the point that your family charity is the ideal venue to intentionally instill rituals and ceremonies that reinforce its vision and mission.

I encourage my clients to invest their efforts in defining the long-term goals they want their foundation to accomplish, and to engage younger generation family members in helping define those goals. I also encourage my clients to develop an annual agenda for their charity's advisory board. That agenda sometimes looks much like the order of worship they are provided at a church service, complete with prayers and selected readings.

I have also helped clients create a process that serves as a rite of passage ritual for young family members who are expected to attend their first foundation advisory board meeting and be prepared to play an active role in making recommendations for charitable contributions. Many of our clients choose to have their foundation board meetings on Thanksgiving Day to underscore the significance of that holiday as an opportunity to express gratitude. However you choose to do it, when younger family members have an emotional connection to the mission of the foundation, the likelihood that it will serve as a lasting multi-generational tool to enhance the family brand and foster a mindset of generosity will be greatly enhanced.

A Giving Strategy is a Recruiting Tool for Employers

I mentioned Alexandre Mars' book in the last chapter. In that book, Mars also observes that there is a clearly discernable generational shift in thinking in Generations Y and Z. These new generations are far more attuned to their desire for purpose and meaning in their lives. It is probably surprising to those of us who are older, but these young people want to know they are working for a business that is conscious of the social impact of its products and services. It is common now to have young people ask potential employers during a job interview about the company's philanthropy initiatives. They want to work for a company that provides a venue for them to participate in making a positive contribution to the world. Business was once all about the bottom-line, but that is no longer true. Talk to human resource directors and they will confirm what I am saying here. This shift is now forcing companies to become aware of their new role in society and adapt to it if they want to attract the best talent.

Use Tax-Wise Strategies to Turbo-Charge Your Charitable Giving

If you have an IRA or other tax qualified retirement account, that account is the ideal source from which to provide endowment funds to your charity or your charitable foundation at your death. If your heirs inherit your tax-qualified accounts, they will not be able to take funds out of the account without paying income tax at ordinary rates on the distribution. There are strategies that allow them to delay the taxation of the withdrawals, but they cannot avoid the tax forever. However, if your tax qualified accounts pass directly to charity, 100% of the funds go to the charity and the income tax is entirely avoided. If your estate is large enough to be subject to the estate tax, that tax can also be avoided on the portion of your IRA that you leave to charity. Many of our clients see gifting their IRA account to their family charity as actually making a gift to their heirs—it's just a different kind of gift.

There are a variety of strategies that make charitable giving more tax efficient and more powerful. One of the most common is the use of charitable remainder trusts (CRTs). This strategy is time-tested and approved by the IRS as long as their guidelines are followed. With a CRT, it is possible to eliminate the capital gains tax on the sale of an asset such as real estate, a business or publicly traded stock. The donor retains an annuity for his or her lifetime (or for joint or even multiple lifetimes) and then, upon the death of the annuity recipients, the remaining amounts in the CRT pass to a charity the donor chooses.

The tax benefits of a charitable remainder trust are substantial, and, in many cases, the economic value of the tax savings will fund the purchase of enough life insurance to leave family members a death benefit that provides an inheritance equal to the inheritance they would have received if they had inherited the asset. In this way, the family is not disadvantaged and the donor's charity or family foundation receives a substantial endowment. There are a number of interesting charitable tax planning strategies available today. These strategies need to be put in place before contracts to sell an asset are signed or in the case of real estate, before listing agreements are signed with a realtor. If you are thinking of selling an appreciated asset, it is wise to consult counsel before you sign any real estate listing agreements or legal documents.

From Small Acorns, Large Trees Grow

I encourage our clients to get started on their generosity plan now and not make the mistake of waiting until they have more time or more money. By starting now, you can engage your family creatively in the process while you are young enough to fully enjoy the activity. You can build your generosity plan around your own need for connection and your passion to make the world a better place. If you start now, it can become a meaningful part of the rest of your life and continue to make a difference for generations after you're gone.

Some great things have started small. The world famous St. Jude's Children's Research Hospital in Memphis was founded by an out of work actor who was essentially broke when he first made the commitment that eventually resulted in this remarkable facility. Onesky.org is a global charity that has transformed the lives of many thousands of marginalized children and helped China to reimagine its entire child welfare system. It was inspired by one California couple—Jenny and Richard Bowen—who had adopted a child from China and saw first-hand the lack of care the country's orphan children received.

My friend Lawson Baker became a widower at age twenty-eight when his wife Cynthia, who had come to the United States from her native Peru for dental school, died suddenly and unexpectedly. I remember quite clearly how, only weeks earlier, she carved the most remarkable Halloween pumpkins on our patio. Cynthia had become passionate about a Peruvian children's charity that provides care and education for special needs children in Latin America. While working his way through the grief of loss, Lawson immersed himself in the mission of this charity—*Manos Unidas*. He now spends a substantial portion of his time leading fundraising efforts in the United States and volunteering with children in Peru, and the charity has grown and thrived because of his leadership.

These are just three examples of what can happen when people with passion step up and take action. The generosity impulse can be ignited by many different sparks—tragedy, compassion or the realization that our lives are missing something essential. The time will never be exactly right; the conditions will never be perfect. My advice is to start anyway. Remarkable things will happen, but only after you take the first step.

Tools for Creating Your Own Generosity Plan

I know that starting with a blank sheet of paper or computer screen can be a challenge. Our friends at Celebrations of Life in Minneapolis have developed a workbook called *Making a Difference Plan: Your Legacy of Generosity*. This booklet makes the process of creating your own generosity plan much easier.

In this booklet, the authors help you identify the issues that matter to you, and they provide you with a template for creating your own plan. I have provided the link to this booklet as well as links to several other useful resources in the resource links to this chapter.

★★★★★★★★★★

Family foundations are an under-utilized tool for building family unity and instilling values in younger generation family members. You should not be intimidated when you consider creating a foundation for your family. The resources in the link below will provide the information you need to get started and follow through. I have also provided links to Manos Unidos, OneSky and St. Jude's Children's Research Center. These are included to illustrate the amazing things individuals can do when they have a vision.

www.YourAmericanLegacy.com/resources

YOUR AMERICAN LEGACY

"No good movie is too long and no bad movie is short enough."

—ROGER EBERT

CHAPTER TWENTY-TWO

Use Movies and Other Media to Share Important Values

From Dashed Olympic Dreams to Hollywood

James Stovall was an Olympic class weight lifter and had won a place on the U. S. Olympic team to compete in the Moscow games in 1980. Unfortunately, that was the same year the Russians decided to invade Afghanistan. In protest, the U.S. boycotted the Olympics. Not long after, Stovall was diagnosed with an eye condition that would inevitably lead to permanent blindness. Today, he lives in Tulsa, and is the author of almost thirty inspirational books, three of which have been made into motion pictures. *The Ultimate Gift, The Ultimate Life* and *Legacy* are films that make the process of sharing important values with younger generation family members an enjoyable entertainment experience.

Films are the modern day version of the ancient art of storytelling which I discussed in Chapter Fourteen. For many parents or grandparents, watching a DVD or ordering a movie on a streaming service or cable is the easiest and most convenient way to share quality time with children or grandchildren and instill important messages at the same time. Of course, the film has to engage everyone's interest, but the options are extensive. Many of the films you always thought of as great often turn out to be films that also communicate powerful values. My wife and I have our own favorites, some of which date back many decades. *The Ten Commandments, Exodus, To Kill a Mockingbird* and *It's a Wonderful Life* are good examples. Some of our favorites are more recent. *Antwone Fisher* is based on a true story. In the film, we see how difficult and how important it was for an intelligent, successful son to reconnect with a mother who had abandoned him. I still think the reunion meeting with his biological mother is the most compelling five minutes of cinema I've ever seen. I can hear him asking his drug-addicted mother who is living in a crack house, "I want to know. Tell me! Why didn't you love me? Why did you give me away?"

It is now also possible to easily access old television series on streaming services. Some of the older series like *The Andy Griffith Show, The Lone Ranger, Have Gun Will Travel,* and *Bonanza* were scripted to include subtle life lessons. That type of programming is not fashionable now, but these old series may still engage the interest of younger children.

I have become a consumer of podcasts. My daily commute to work takes about the same amount of time as several of the podcasts to which I subscribe. Because podcasts are inexpensive to produce, there are an endless range of choices available. Some of the best ones are free. My wife and I are both fans of Michael Hyatt's *Lead to Win* podcast.

There are dozens of films, television series, inspirational websites, and podcasts that can be useful in connecting younger generations with the values that matter to you. You may already have your favorites. I have included some in the resources link on our website. I have tried our list out on people of different ages, including some very self-aware twenty-somethings, and while some of the films and TV series on the list can be a bit preachy, that is not the case with many of them. I have done my best to make the task of choosing the right one easy for you. I keep this list updated. I also appreciate recommendations that should be added, so please email me and allow me to share them with our community.

Explore the list of suggested movies, television programs, podcasts and other media in the link below. My team and I have organized this list into categories that will help you choose a resource that is appropriate for the audience. Some of the movies have an "R" rating, but we thought they were worthy of inclusion because of the power of the message they communicate. Just be careful you have the right audience. The list of resources for this chapter could be much longer. Let me know if you have one I should add.

www.YourAmericanLegacy.com/resources

YOUR AMERICAN LEGACY

"Show me a family of readers, and I will show you the people that move the world."

—Napoleon Bonaparte

CHAPTER TWENTY-THREE

Read Books, Especially Aloud

William Bennett was the Secretary of Education in the Reagan Administration. He often visited schools during his tenure. Bennett later explained that in those visits, he had conversations with teachers who expressed difficulty in communicating common moral principles to diverse student bodies. He proposed the rather ancient notion that one of the most effective ways to communicate moral values to younger generations was to read aloud to them from literature that communicated those values. This idea is very similar to the idea I mentioned in Chapter Fourteen where I point out that storytelling is the ancient, time-tested way to communicate important values. Reading books aloud is the more recent version of storytelling; It became commonplace in the Eighteenth Century when literacy became commonplace.

In 1993, Bennett wrote an anthology called *The Book of Virtues: A Treasury of Great Moral Stories*. The book is divided into chapters on different virtues including self-discipline, compassion, responsibility, friendship, work, courage, perseverance, honesty, loyalty, and faith. If those are values that are important for you to share, Bennett has done the homework for you.

The idea of reading aloud from literature is as useful and effective today as it was two hundred years ago—perhaps more so. In a fascinating new book titled *The Enchanted Hour: The Miraculous Power of Reading Aloud in the Age of Distraction*, author Meghan Cox Gurdon argues that reading aloud to our children and to each other is a fast-working antidote to fractured attention spans as technology pulls us in the opposite direction. Here is more of what she has to say: "A miraculous alchemy occurs when one person reads to another, transforming the simple stuff of a book, a voice and a bit of time into complex and powerful fuel for the heart, brain and imagination." I completely buy what she is saying. My wife and I read to our sons when they were young and we read aloud to each other now. On road trips, we have an agreement that she drives and I do the reading. When we can't read together, we make notes and flag pages we later share with each other.

With the increased availability of options for audio books, road trips and long plane flights have become an educational opportunity. Whether you read alone or aloud with others, books continue to be a great way to create a deeper personal connection, learn new things and share values.

My team and I have organized a fairly extensive list of books that will make the task of choosing appropriate reading content easier. I have not included references to foundational religious texts, partly because those works are so well known and partly because I am not familiar with every religion and did not want to inadvertently omit relevant sources. There is a link to Meghan Cox Gurdon's new book The Enchanted Hour: The Miraculous Power of Reading Aloud in the Age of Distraction.

www.YourAmericanLegacy.com/resources

PART 4

Fini: What is the True Measure of Success?

In this book, I have introduced a framework for how to think about your legacy as well as a wide range of practical tools you can use to create it. A fair question to ask at this point is: How will I know I have succeeded? I think it's important to have clarity around the answer to that question. Of course, you never intend to reach a defining end-point where your legacy stops expanding. I fully expect the stories, traditions, and values that matter to us will continue to be infused in each new generation. But there will likely be defining moments in the lives of your family members or in the life of the family as a unit when the quality of your efforts will be tested. You may not be here to witness it when it happens, but that shouldn't matter. I know the measure of success will be different for every individual and every family. In the final chapter, I share my personal answer to that question.

"You see, idealism detached from action is just a dream. But idealism allied with pragmatism, with rolling up your sleeves and making the world bend a bit, is very exciting. It's very real. It's very strong."

—BONO

"All good men and women must take responsibility to create legacies that will take the next generation to a level we could only imagine."

—JIM ROHN

CHAPTER TWENTY-FOUR

Our American Legacy

An Inspired Idea

In 1863, the United States was mired in a civil war that had killed tens of thousands of young Americans. Earlier, in July of that year, the Battle of Gettysburg created over 46,000 additional casualties as the conflict continued to grind on with no end in sight. In October of that year, President Lincoln did something that— given the dark cloud of conflict hanging over the country—seemed so counterintuitive, his action had to be divinely inspired. By declaration, he created a new American holiday that was established for the sole purpose of carving out an entire day for Americans to celebrate their gratitude for the blessings and bounties, which, as Lincoln put it, were of "so extraordinary a nature, that they cannot fail to penetrate and soften even the heart." It was an extraordinary idea—a day dedicated to giving thanks created in the depths of the costliest war America has ever fought.

Who Will Come to Thanksgiving Dinner after You're Gone?

Thanksgiving is a uniquely American holiday. For most of us, it's about who will be responsible for the turkey and who will bring the sweet potato casserole. It's also about watching football and drifting off to sleep during the game under the influence of tryptophan and massive amounts of carbohydrates.

Over the last thirty years, many of the clients I've met with share a desire to reduce their taxes and keep their business affairs out of court. Other issues are important to them too, like paying for the cost of long-term care, protecting spouses if they remarry, and protecting children from divorce or financial immaturity. In recent years, however, I am sure I am hearing something more, something that goes to the heart of who we are as a people. Something we might think of as transcendent or spiritual.

More than any other thing, what I am hearing is a desire to know their family will remain close, love each other and take care of each other. Put simply, we all want to know our family will continue to share Thanksgiving dinner after we are gone. Protecting wealth is important, but the most important thing is knowing family members will continue speaking to each other, loving and caring about each other, spending time together, supporting each other when there are struggles and challenges, and celebrating together when there are victories. I would like for my success as a parent to be measured by that standard. I believe the success of my work as a professional should be measured by how well my work has influenced families to have that kind of success.

From Moscow to Minnesota

I boarded a connecting flight in Atlanta early one morning and sat down in the aisle seat. Just as the doors were about to close, a young man who had just barely made his connection sat down in the seat next to mine. I learned he had just arrived in the United States on an overnight flight from Moscow. He had not slept for at least a day, but he was alive with excitement. He had an engineering degree and a dream of coming to America. He had won the visa lottery that allowed him to work for a family in Minnesota that sold snow cones at county fairs.

I asked, "Why did you want to come to America?"

He didn't hesitate. "I come to America," he said, "because in America I can become self-made man."

Every day, all around the world, smart, ambitious young people line up at our embassies to sign up for the chance to win the visa lottery and have the opportunity to find some menial job in America that could give them the foothold they need to become a self-made man or woman in the one country that is the defining symbol of opportunity.

I am proud of my country. I am encouraged that motivated people continue to be inspired by everything the torch in the hands of the Statue of Liberty represents. I want to know that torch is in good hands when I am no longer here. When we nurture the next generation, when we instill them with faith, a work ethic, integrity, and generosity, our country will be more prosperous, safer and more secure. When we do that, we can know our country will be in the right hands when we are no longer here to serve.

That is the American legacy I want.

Join me. We can do this.

★★★★★★★★★★

*Thanksgiving has become my favorite holiday. I need—we all need—
an occasion to think about the importance of generosity in our lives. I
am still amazed that President Lincoln had the wisdom to make this
a national holiday in the most depressing time of the Civil War. Read
more about Lincoln's decision in the link below. I have also included
a link to the U. S. Visa Lottery. The number of individuals who
actually obtain a green card is less than 1% of those who apply. I
have provided a link that explains how the visa lottery process works,
primarily to underscore the gratitude American should feel to be born
into a country that people around the world work for years to come to.*

www.USAFamilyLegacy.com

Learn More About Thanksgiving and Generosity

Epilogue

Our team at Legacy Advisors and Project Perseverance sincerely hope that you have enjoyed reading Your *American Legacy*.

We trust that within these pages, you have discovered some valuable insights and suggestions that can help put you on track towards leaving a lasting legacy to those who are important to you. Through the years we have been privileged to work with many outstanding people who were once in your very shoes! They wanted to take the necessary steps to begin building and then leaving something of lasting worth and importance.

The good news is that you are ahead of the game, so-to-speak, because you have this book in your possession. It is a great jumping-off point towards building something lasting so that loved ones can look back at your time spent on earth as something extremely meaningful. Plus, for you, it is an opportunity to leave an impactful lasting impression on those you wish to guide and direct towards having better lives.

When you think about it, our time on earth is short, in relation to the vast reaches of the days, weeks, months and years the planet has existed. Because of this, we have to do something that can far extend our physical existence. Our spouse, children, grandchildren and their children will be able to look back with pride on what you have accomplished and left for others to experience.

For over 25 years, we have been at the forefront of providing the kind of guidance which has enabled many great people to put their mark on the world. We look forward to being of service, and ask: will you be our next success story in leaving *Your American Legacy*?

We have authored several books and provided discovery sessions in our communities to Protect Families for Generations. Your American Legacy is a vital resource to provide you peace of mind in the post Covid world. We hope our discovery resources enable you to protect your family for generations.

From Dennis B. Sullivan Esq, CPA, LLM, MS Mgt and our team, "We are standing by, ready to protect you and your family for generations"

SHARE YOUR LEGACY JOURNEY

We'd love to hear about your legacy journey and connect you with a community of like-minded advisors, family members and resources that might be helpful to you as you plan your own legacy journey. Visit our website at *USAFamilyLegacy.com* where you can sign up for our newsletter and receive notice of news, workshops and upcoming projects.

Made in the USA
Middletown, DE
15 September 2023